SELLING ON THE FAST TRACK

SELLING ON THE FAST TRACK

How to Become a Sales Athlete®

Kathy Aaronson

G. P. PUTNAM'S SONS
NEW YORK

G. P. Putnam's Sons
Publishers Since 1838
200 Madison Avenue
New York, NY 10016

Published simultaneously in Canada

Library of Congress Cataloging-in-Publication Data
Aaronson, Kathy.
Selling on the fast track: how to become a Sales Athlete/by Kathy Aaronson.
p. cm.
1. Selling. I. Title.
HF5438.25.A22 1989 88-32356 CIP
658.8′5—dc19
ISBN 0-399-13461-1

Designed by Beth Tondreau Design/Gabrielle Hamberg

Printed in the United States of America
1 2 3 4 5 6 7 8 9 10

To Helen Gurley Brown for being the best role model a woman could ever have. To Walt Disney for his special ability to inspire love and admiration in everyone everywhere. To my husband, Thomas, for teaching me to teach people about cutting seven-figure deals—fairly.

Acknowledgments

Don Neece, Mike O'Brien, Nancy Martini, Ann Bancroft, Welles Miller, Beth Watt, Carol Ann Lyons, Bob Lieb, Betty Harris, Lindley Boegehold, Tina Isaac, Jack Artenstein, David W. King

Contents

CONTENTS

Foreword

When I joined Crain's Chicago Business ten years ago as publisher, I had been a crime reporter, financial writer and marketing columnist for daily newspapers. I worked on the editorial side of publishing, a business where editorial people and advertising sales people don't talk. They usually sneer at each other.

After going through a rigorous on-the-job

training program, I learned a lot about sales, the hard way.

When I met Kathy Aaronson. POW! It hit me. This was the mentor I should have known ten years ago. I could have saved myself a lot of sweat and grief. Here in one neatly tied package I could have shaved years off my training. Kathy has the right attitudes and the right standards to generate sales success. And her concept of the Sales Athlete® is brilliant.

Sales athletes are as far ahead of the non-professionals as NBA players are ahead of schoolyard basketball jocks.

That's why Kathy Aaronson is my nominee for Coach of the Year.

Joe Cappo
GROUP PUBLISHER
CRAIN'S COMMUNICATIONS

(CRAIN'S CHICAGO BUSINESS, CRAIN'S NEW YORK BUSINESS, ADVERTISING AGE, CITY & STATE MAGAZINE, ELECTRONIC MEDIA, CRAIN'S BUSINESS IN THE AIR [AMERICAN AIRLINES], PENSIONS & INVESTMENT AGE)

PART I

The Anatomy of a Sales Athlete

Introduction

I started selling because I'd had enough. For the previous five years, I had watched other people become successful at something I was born to do—sell. I was working three jobs, trying to climb the corporate ladder as a fashion buyer, when a salesman from *Cosmopolitan* magazine called on me and let it slip that his salary was twice as much as my combined earnings.

Within weeks, I had secured a position on the sales staff of *Cosmopolitan* magazine and was knocking on the doors of Madison Avenue and delivering my new script enthusiastically:

"Hi, I'm young, I'm single, and if you want to reach a girl like me, you'll find me reading *Cosmopolitan.*"

It worked. I had no idea why—I just seemed lucky. The memories of grueling hours at half the pay remained fresh, however, and I feared the luck wouldn't last. I was determined to decode the "luck" I'd had in sales—so I'd never have to look back.

I began my training program with the most successful salespeople at the Hearst Publishing Company, the corporate owners of *Cosmopolitan.* These were the top salespeople at *Good Housekeeping, Harper's Bazaar, House Beautiful, Town & Country* and *Eye* magazine. They were the kind of salespeople I would later describe as sales athletes.

I met a mentor, O.B. Bond, publisher of *Eye* magazine, who trained me to understand how my prospects sold their products—from stereos to liquor, automobiles to ideas. Then he taught me how to sell them advertising.

In eleven years of selling advertising to sales managers, marketing directors and presidents of some of the most successful corporations in the world and also some of the least successful, I established an invaluable overview of how people sell. I met sales athletes in every major industry.

I enjoyed these people. They were smart, ethical, generous, energetic, successful and at ease with their success. As I trained myself through their examples, I worked to break down and share with others the keys to career satisfaction, success and security.

I went on to become a founding member of *Girl Talk* magazine, advertising manager and associate publisher of *Women's Wear Daily*'s consumer publication *W* and marketing consultant for *Working Woman* magazine. Liz Smith's gossip column referred to me as a "publishing genius." I was twenty-six years old.

The career that began with that Cosmopolitan Girl developed into a richly rewarding lifestyle in which business and pleasure are virtually inseparable.

When the day came that employers were willing to pay me the equivalent of a year's salary for part-time work, I launched a career in training, developing and counseling sales athletes. I moved over the years from selling magazine advertising to selling magazine sales staffs—and clients such as Johnson & Johnson, Irving Trust and Revlon—on how I sell.

In the course of training more than two hundred people a week and consulting for corporations ranging from television networks to forklift manufacturers, I have been struck by the similarities in sales athletes. I've found that only about one in every two hundred people has an instinctive understanding of the training you'll receive in this book. Others, by adopting this program, can learn to decode "luck" and train themselves for success.

There is a good job in sales for everyone with

at least average intelligence. You doubt that? Consider that I have facilitated into satisfying sales careers thousands of floundering recent college graduates and hundreds of people making dramatic late-in-life career changes. My program has passed the test of fire in training and directing a sixty-five-year-old retired grammar school principal, former nuns, a recently widowed homemaker and mother of four, a disabled ex-police officer, a former FBI agent.

You don't have to be a "born" salesperson. This book will lead you to greater career and personal satisfaction by telling you *what* to sell, *how* to sell it and how to remain secure by keeping contacts loyal.

CHAPTER 1

The Most Valuable Players (MVPs) in Sales

Regardless of the state of the economy, there are many more great jobs begging for sales athletes than there are sales athletes to fill them. That's why this program works as a sales career strategy in a good or bad economy.

In December of 1981, when the job market had melted down, my sales training and placement service helped more people find good jobs than at any other time. My services expanded to include both customized sales training and consulting to major corporations and governments worldwide. Today, I get calls every day from top companies willing to pay high salaries for the people we call sales athletes.

If you recoil at the thought of "sales"—imagining that selling somehow involves conning innocent people into buying things they don't need—read on. Your basic honesty and sensitivity are qualities that will help you become a sales athlete.

I stress the concept of "athlete" because like a top track or field player, a sales athlete never stops training. As I said, sales athletes aren't born. They are people who have committed themselves to getting into and staying in vocational shape, to living balanced personal and professional lives. Theirs is a lifestyle of building creative strength and problem-solving endurance in order to achieve peak performance. They are passionate and have paid the price it takes to put themselves at the top of their industries—enjoying a professional overview that lets them call the next play.

The similarities in these successful people rest not in their job descriptions, but in the attitude, style and performance strategies they employ. The attributes they share are the qualities that I believe make sales athletes.

The Sales Athlete in Action

1) Sales Athletes Have Passion for Their Work

Of the thousands of people I train every year, many believe they have miscast themselves in their sales careers. In fact, all that stands between their discomfort with selling and a fulfilling sales career is the fact that they don't believe in the products, services or ideas they represent.

"The single greatest quality that separates good people from great is passion," declares Karen Fund, publisher of the nationally acclaimed *LA Style* magazine, who manages a sales athlete staff of twenty-eight.

"One of the things that compels a person's attention to take the time from other responsibilities and listen to you is passion," Fund continues. "Passion is unmistakable, and it's a very attractive quality—people turn on to it."

When I was at *W*, the consumer sister publication of *Women's Wear Daily,* I finally reached the president of a personal computer component company. I'd been trying to contact him for weeks and was very excited about breaking this advertising category to *W*. I knew our readers were the first to buy microwaves, first to buy giant TV screens, would be the first to computerize their homes.

Three weeks later, on the morning of our appointment, a winter storm had shut down most businesses in New York. I decided to go to the appointment anyway. I was so involved in the idea that I couldn't sit home thinking about how to sell more PCs. I took subways and cabs to Brooklyn through the sleet, arrived at the building—and found the front door locked. I went around the building trying all the doorknobs, until I found one that was unlocked. I called out, and a man called back, giving me directions to his office. He looked at me in disbelief. "This is the sign of a leader," he said.

"I couldn't miss our meeting because of weather," I replied. He invited me to remove my wet coat and boots, and offered me a cup of coffee. In the first five minutes of my presentation he agreed that computers were a symbol of fashionable living. For the next four hours we designed his ad, a direct mail campaign to dealers and sales presentations to the leads generated by his campaign. It was the energy born from passion that made that sale.

Sales athletes are hidden in their clients' offices;

you hear about them but rarely see or talk to them. They are invigorated day by day while confidently facing new challenges, new contacts, and servicing existing clients with fresh information. This no-can-lose attitude doesn't come simply from a pep talk they give themselves every morning in front of the mirror. It comes from taking pleasure in knowing they are giving the very best, and it shows.

When you build your career with the Sales Athlete® training, the delight of satisfied clients will ignite your passion. You won't need to pump yourself up with entertaining exercises that have little to do with your sales assignment. The positive reinforcement of clients keeps sales athletes committed to their careers. It spurs their willingness to pay the price needed to overcome beginner's frustrations. This passion for serving clients well makes worthwhile the grueling work of establishing a new territory or career.

"Let's face it, it boils down to hard work," says sales athlete Frank Crupi, the franchiser for Safeguard Business Systems in San Mateo County, California, the number one supplier of business forms. Crupi—a role model and guest sales trainer for the hundreds of Safeguard franchisers—started without a contact base when he relocated to the Bay Area from Washington state. He was willing to pace himself through seven-day work weeks in order to establish a network of satisfied clients.

When I met him at a week-long golf clinic in Carmel, California, he recalled the price he paid to achieve his current lifestyle: "I ate bananas while I drove 60 miles to service a client," he said. "I always put my clients' needs first."

Paying the price for Crupi meant that when his children were tiny and his business just starting, he went to work at 4:30 A.M. and came back home at 7:00 A.M. in order to share breakfast with his family.

Today he continues to pace his life, the same way an athlete learns the discipline of pacing to achieve optimum performance. Happy he paid the price, Crupi now enjoys a four-day work week, a full exercise schedule, active involvement in prestigious social and service clubs and shuttling between his homes on the San Francisco Peninsula and Maui.

For television film producer Doris Keating, paying the price meant seven long years of persistently developing contacts in an industry brutal to newcomers, before getting a crack at her own first production.

"Everybody said, 'How could she hang in there that long?' " says Keating, now the hottest female producer of TV miniseries in Hollywood. "I mean, this is a business that is so rejection-oriented, it's 99 percent rejection."

Passionate to produce "My Wicked, Wicked Ways," the autobiography of Errol Flynn to which she held the rights, Keating wouldn't give up. She knew it was a great idea: she believed in it, was passionate about it, and was willing to pay the price over seven years to take it to the screen.

Relaxing in her elegant Beverly Hills home, surrounded by Chagall prints and served breakfast by a full-time housekeeper, Keating recalled just how she started: "I learned all I know about the industry from reading everything from Sidney Sheldon and Harold Robbins to the *Wall Street Journal* and the *Enquirer* plus every trade publication, as well as picking the brains of people in the industry." Recognizing that people in her industry are anything but eager to give advice to potential competitors, she gained trust and gleaned information by learning the foibles of individual companies, then giving *them* advice.

2) A Sales Athlete Never Burns a Client

Skeptical prospects abound because the reputation of a sales representative is to sell people products they neither need nor want. But rather than push a prospect into a sale, sales athletes "train" prospects in the benefits of their product or service. They are rabid in their quest to meet clients' needs. They don't sell refrigerators to Eskimos. They sell *stoves* to Eskimos. Sales athletes sell clients what they need. Uncovering and satisfying needs is the smart game plan for people who want to succeed in sales.

Reams of articles have been written about the decline of service and product quality in America. Sad to say, people have learned to expect less, rather than more, from products and services. If your tires are supposed to give you 60,000 miles, you're happy to get 30,000. The pantyhose that are supposed to last forever? You consider yourself lucky if they wear five times. The repairman said he'd be there today at 10:00 A.M.? You'll be glad to see him anytime this week. In this kind of environment, people who simply do what they say they are going to do are rare. Sales athletes, however, succeed because they always try to do what they say they are going to do and never knowingly make agreements that they can't keep.

I witnessed a sales athlete in action at the birthday party of a five-year-old. The kids were given Hostess Ring Dings as treats, and as each took a bite, they called out, "Where's the cream filling?" One of the mothers rushed quickly to the phone and called Hostess. Within the hour, a uniformed, official-looking delivery man arrived with Hostess gifts galore. Imagine the look on those children's faces as he explained: "We don't know how this could have happened because each Ring Ding is weighed before packaging, but we hope you and your friends will enjoy a Hostess happy birthday." The look on the faces of those children is the look I work to create on the faces of my clients when, despite the best of intentions, things go awry.

If you heed only this one rule consistently, I'm convinced you'll still enjoy a competitive edge: Always do what you say you will do, and do it when you say you will do it.

3) Sales Athletes Are Executive Communicators

They know what it takes to establish rapport and lower the resistance of whomever they need to communicate with, whether that person is affably interested or rude and abrasive. They possess an ability to inspire others, and the patience to communicate with people who are nowhere near as masterfully communicative. Their communication style is clear, positive and friendly.

Sales athletes are tenacious as bulldogs in pursuit of new business, but they never achieve success through intimidation or obnoxious, scripted spiels. They are able quickly to gauge the style and communications abilities of those around them, to listen fully, put others at ease and inspire trust. To do this, they must frequently set aside their own emotional blocks to successful communication.

Even gregarious salespeople may fear approaching others without prearranged appointments, or have problems communicating confidently with certain types of people. A person who is comfortable approaching a secretary, for example, may have to overcome anxiety or insecurity when communicating with the president of a major company.

Your mother may not have known you would want to go into sales, and perhaps you grew up with a fear of authority. Sales athletes know when it's time to leave behind them emotional reactions learned in childhood. They surround themselves with communicators—in the media and in their own profession—collecting solutions and ideas that will inspire the people they do business with. By attuning themselves to the needs of their contacts, communicating with honesty and sensitivity, sales athletes win confidence. Once they have inspired trust, they are tenacious and assertive in communicating the value of the product, service or idea being sold.

Ute Lawrence, publisher of *London Magazine* in Ontario, Canada, was faced with selling advertising at the height of a recession in that manufacturing city. As she called on retailers, she noticed they all responded to "How are you today?" with a litany of discouraging news about the economy. At the same time, the city was filled with tourists and business travelers, all of whom turned to her magazine as an official guide to local retail stores and restaurants. Determined to stop the downward spiral, Ute met one-on-one with businesspeople, at chamber of commerce and association meetings, spreading the word that the London sky was not falling, and literally turned around the negative self-perception that was scaring customers away. She inspired an entire town when times were tough, and is looked upon today as a leader in the community.

4) Sales Athletes Are Well-Equipped

Any tools that help prioritize activities, target associations and move past fear are included in the equipment of a sales athlete.

Sales athletes recognize that if you are computerphobic today, you are on the bench, out of the game. They are comfortable with laptop computers and electronic maps, and understand how to use voice networks and fax equipment. By staying on top of technology, they work toward a shorter, more productive day. For a stockbroker, basic equipment might be a portable Quotron that sends up-to-the-minute stock prices via satellite, plus a car phone, a custom-tailored suit and more than one reliable secretary. For an advertising executive it may consist of a Mercedes, a Chanel suit and an impeccably crafted media kit. Today, salespeople are linked to data processing centers and can be provided with faxed contracts for signature before they conclude a sales presentation, or a satellite system to help them move through traffic.

Don't get discouraged if you're just starting out and think such expensive equipment is beyond your means. You won't be knocked out of the box simply because you drive a Chevy instead of a Mercedes. The most important equipment, as we'll discuss more fully in Chapter 3, is that which helps you prioritize your activities, gather information and target your relationships: It includes magazines, newspapers and books that keep up with the cutting edge in sales, marketing and specific industries. It should always include the books currently being read by your clients, so you can establish easy rapport through shared information resources.

Many sales athletes have told me how mind-expanding programs, including subliminal tapes, have helped them remove emotional blocks to their success.

A good wardrobe also belongs on your list of essential equipment. Your clothing should be neither pinstriped conservative nor trendy; rather, it should give you the appearance of your client's best customer.

And how do you feel about driving your car up to a valet at the most fashionable restaurant in town? Do you have a clean, well-maintained vehicle that can safely get you from one appointment to the next?

Equipment may also mean the best seats at a

baseball game to which you've invited a client. Or reservations for the best table at the best restaurant in town. A sales athlete's equipment helps convey the overall idea that "nobody does it better." (See "The Equipment of a Sales Athlete" on p. 219.)

5) Sales Athletes Enjoy Creative Problem-Solving

"Problems? What problems? I *look* for problems," says Merrill Brown, a thirty-year sales athlete who represents the Crane Paper Company in thirteen western states and Canada. It is Brown's ability to tackle the challenge of problem-solving with eagerness that engenders the loyalty of his customers. His clients turn to him first, even in this extremely competitive field, where all products are essentially the same and business is won through the quality of the presentation.

The ability to solve problems creatively comes first from preparing yourself thoroughly by gathering all the information available to help you reach your goal, then by sorting or editing that information and using it to develop a fresh idea that best fits the needs of your client prospects. If you do this, you'll find that the fun of work is solving problems.

A sales athlete may be part of an industry in crisis. While others in the industry enmesh themselves in the problem, the sales athlete looks outside of the normal industry-wide channels to gather the information and methods necessary to get beyond the problem and move ahead. Without revealing trade secrets, the sales athlete circulates through his clients' industries, gathering and sharing with clients all of the fresh information necessary to maintaining a competitive edge. Consider the respect won by Lee Iacocca for his renowned problem-solving skills.

At a time when American auto manufacturers were barely surviving Japanese competition, Iacocca sold the U.S. Congress, the president and the American people on the idea of bailing out the Chrysler Motor Company. He then made good on his word, bringing Chrysler back to profitability and repaying every cent to the government. In a country where the car industry as a whole is mistrusted, Iacocca has sold us on his ethics and on his cars. He is one of the most revered sales athlete in America.

If you are someone who honestly gets a great deal of happiness out of solving other people's problems, that's the difference between making $25,000 the hard way and earning $100,000 a year while loving every minute. Sales athletes run toward the problems of clients and client prospects, not away from them. Sales athletes feel great about solving problems because of the positive feedback they continually receive. It helps them get beyond their own fear and self-doubt in order to reach solutions analytically.

6) Sales Athletes See, Understand and Attain Prospect and Client Goals

"Most people I hire are tacticians," says Debra Turner, a top marketing executive for DHL Courier Co. "They are tactically sound. You put out a strategy for them, identify where they are going and where the end result is, and tactically they get there. The cream of the crop, though, are strategists. Those are the sales athletes—the ones who can approach a new situation and develop a strategy to fit it." They ask questions, they listen, they see, understand, and move their products, services and ideas into place to meet the goals of their clients. It is those strategists, according to Turner, who are able to earn $50,000 in their first year with her company, and "shoot up the ladder really fast."

Sales athletes employ this "overview" perspective when laying out their own career strategies. Look at your game plan: Do you see the whole game, or just the last play completed and the next?

When I first started seriously dating the man who is now my husband, a successful rock music manager, he said, "I'm going to travel 80 percent of the time over the next three years. Bear with me, because when I am done, I will know the people I need to know—every record retailer, wholesaler and distributor, major promoter, radio programmer and record label representative in the country."

He saw, understood and attained that goal, building a latticework of contacts that enables him to know exactly who buys records and seats to concerts and who listens to radio. Today, because of this carefully executed overview, he is considered a visionary in the entertainment industry.

7) Sales Athletes Have Balanced Personal and Professional Lives

What's more important to you—your professional or personal life? That was a trick question. What should be most important is your professional *and* personal life. To succeed in business, you need an overview of your industry. To succeed in life, you need an overview of your life—a broad awareness of your own priorities and goals for health, relationships and financial well-being.

Marilyn Bixler, a sales athlete for a chemical company, was offered a promotion and relocation to corporate headquarters in Northern California. One day, three months after she relocated, she called me to say she was miserable. Her company retained my services to help her become better acclimated to her new home. As I tried to discern the problems with her territory, it became clear to me that the issue was not professional but personal. She was lonely. She missed her health club, her "perfect hamburger," her local shopping area with friendly merchants who knew her name.

That day Marilyn went to work as usual—and I became a scout, canvassing the city to find replacements for those important personal connections she'd lost. Late that afternoon I picked her up at her office, and introduced her to her new city.

Marilyn, a conscientious worker, had taken her personal life for granted. Once I pointed out the locations—a lively hamburger restaurant, a health club and cozy neighborhood of shops and services—she made a point of frequenting them and establishing new relationships. I turned her on to singles meetings at the church of her denomination, a discount florist because she loves flowers, and business associations that held meetings where she could network. Now Marilyn puts back at the end of every day what the job has taken out of her. She loves her new city, her job, her balanced life.

Pacing is crucial in the training and lifestyle of sales athletes. They neither avoid work nor burn out on it, and they seek a healthy balance in striving toward both personal and professional goals.

Frequently, they "work" many more hours than the average nine-to-fiver, but that is because much of their business involves enjoying time with clients away from the office. They find ways to bring clients and their children together with their own families, and balance work with pleasure while doing business. They have created careers for themselves that meet their own needs for work with people and away from them, and that allow them to associate with people they like.

8) Sales Athletes Develop a Support System of Experts and Mentors

Helen Gurley Brown was one of my first mentors. We share rural backgrounds. She first became an accessible role model to me twenty years ago. It was at her birthday party, when I was too shy to sing a solo "Happy Birthday," that Brown first gave me comfort and encouraged me to get over my fear by tackling public speaking engagements.

The sales athlete develops a quality support system of experts and mentors, just as any athlete has a coach and trainer. Mentors are people who are already doing what you want to be doing. They help you remove self-doubt by showing you clearly that what you seek is within your grasp.

My own support system today includes a vast assortment of people ranging from insurance agents, wordsmiths, fashion trendsetters, politicians, power brokers and editors to thousands of sales athletes, rabbis, ministers, an exercise trainer and my family. These are people whom I've met and who have been kind and helpful to me over the past sixteen years of my career. All of them are still accessible to me and, although I don't "use" them, knowing they exist as a support network gives me the courage and the freedom to take risks. In return, I gladly place the might of my organization and its contacts and goodwill behind these people when they have problems and need my resources.

By looking through the eyes of mentors who have "been there" before, you are able to gain an accurate and broad overview of your professional life. With this overview, sales athletes are able to quarterback their careers intelligently.

9) Sales Athletes Know the Competition

Sales athletes stand toe-to-toe with their competitors, look them in the eye and identify their weaknesses. Once you get to know your own toughest competitors, they'll no longer inspire awe—or fear—in you. Like Frank Crupi, you'll be able to say, "There is no competition—only interference."

Knowing the competition means knowing their best clients, why those clients do business with them and when their contracts are up for renegotiation.

The sales athlete uses creativity, sophisticated skills in time management and account targeting to spot the hole in the competitor's defense. When the time is right, the sales athlete is ready to leap in and win the account.

10) Sales Athletes Are Socially Astute

Selling is a social skill. People do business with the people most like them. People recognize each other by familiarity with their overall physical presentation. Words simply are not enough. If you want your clients to like you, you must know how to send the signals that *show* you like them.

In a successful sales career, you will develop relationships and take them with you from year to year. Doing that requires that you develop social skills, not only for the office, but at breakfast meetings, luncheons, cocktail parties, club functions and sporting events. You can never afford to be socially awkward.

Linda Carpenter, manager of business development at Paramount Motion Pictures, was discussing a "power" dinner party at which one guest proved to be so socially obnoxious he aroused in her what she described as an "allergic reaction."

The man was physically well built, well-dressed and worldly in most aspects. However, he literally invaded the "personal space" of Linda and other guests at the party. He loomed above them—speaking from just inches away—and moved closer as they stepped back. His lack of sensitivity prompted Linda and the other guests to declare they would never invite him anywhere again. The man had wiped himself out of this elite group.

Being socially astute means understanding preferred seating, and knowing how to provide a client with the most fun he's ever had with a business associate. It involves attention to crucial details as well: understanding the etiquette of where to put the napkin when you leave the table for a phone call, when to pay cash, when to order a drink and when not to, when to use a credit card and when to leave.

Being socially astute also involves patience—the patience to truly listen to your clients' needs, to wait rather than interrupt and to adjust your timing to the timing of your clients.

After one of my clients lamented to me how difficult it was to find places to take her three children and how few people invite children to their homes, I planned a party for her and her children that would include my other clients with their children, since I felt they too might share her problem.

I hired a magician to entertain the clients and their kids. The hometown newspapers of my clients were there, and major sports events were aired on three television sets. The point was to create as many different experiences as I could for people to share.

How did I benefit? I cemented relationships with these clients, who stumbled over each other with stories of how successful my Sales Athlete® training program had been for their business.

The Sales Athlete® Training Program

Now that you've met the sales athlete, it's time to introduce you to the Sales Athlete® training program. Begin by customizing the training to your specific needs with the help of this simple true-or-false test:

I. I have been trained to:
- a) Select a sales career path.
- b) Identify the type of executive sales position most satisfying to me.
- c) Get a great sales job.

II. I have been trained to:
- a) Manage my time effectively.
- b) Target accounts.
- c) Access key decision-makers.
- d) Give one-on-one presentations.
- e) Give presentations to from 3 to 200 people.
- f) Close a sale.

III. I have been trained to:
- a) Renew client agreements.

b) Nurture contacts year to year.
c) Entertain business associates.

The premise of this test is to uncover areas with which you are unfamiliar. You are most likely to experience fear or inhibition in those areas where you answered "false." This fear will always inhibit your achieving the goals you or your manager have established for your career. The opposite of fear, I believe, is familiarity.

The test is keyed to the various sections of this book. If you answered "false" to questions in section I of the test, turn to Chapter 2 for help with career selection. If any of your responses were "false" in section II, turn to Chapters 3 through 6 for tips on career satisfaction. If you answered "false" to questions in section III of the test, read Chapters 7 and 8 for strengthening your sense of career security. Take yourself through the Sales Athlete® training program step-by-step by reading the whole book. Then go back for brush-up training where needed.

PART II

Career Satisfaction

WHAT TO SELL

CHAPTER 2

Choosing the Right Arena

The Sales Athlete® program includes guidance in career selection and sales training. It is a what-to-sell-and-how-to-sell-it program. Sales athletes choose their arenas carefully. They don't leave this decision to the luck of the draw, to the Help Wanted section of a newspaper or to an acquaintance with a "once-in-a-lifetime opportunity."

Far too many people would like to think of job hunting like this: You walk into an elevator and loudly proclaim, "I'm looking for a job." Someone says, "We've got one on the third floor." You get out on the third floor, ask for your desk and sit down. You then ask the person next to you, "By the way, how much does it pay?" And so what if it's $1,000 less than the last job—as long as you didn't have to keep looking.

Sales athletes search for the right job with the same creative effort and positive, self-confident attitude they put into developing a new account. A small price to pay, when you consider that your career *and* lifestyle are at stake.

The arena for your career should be chosen on the basis of:

- Who you would like to do business with ultimately.
- What contact base you would like to nurture and take with you throughout your career.
- How you would prefer to access these people.
- How complex or simple a sales project you want to undertake. In other words, how frequently do you need the satisfaction of a result? Sales are frequent in retail, infrequent when you sell jet planes.
- What managerial structure is most conducive to your success. Your manager will be your coach. Do you learn better in a highly structured, disciplined environment, or with someone who is only there when you need support? Very few people have the ability to train themselves.

It's your life, your career. Don't leave things to

chance. Start now making your own choices by identifying the industry and the sales communications style and career best suited to *you*—one that will provide you with increasing income and security. Then, *you* do the interviewing to find the job that's best suited to you.

There is a sales job out there for everyone. I don't doubt this. I am, however, concerned about the possible mortality of your sales career. I urge you to protect your business reputation and your contact base so that, if your company merges, or if a market shift in technology in your field occurs through no fault of your own, you are not trapped at age fifty-seven. With your Sales Athlete® strategy in place, you can move easily from one job to the next regardless of academic credentials, location or age.

An Air Force colonel in his late fifties retired with no idea of how to find a job, because the U.S. government had been his only employer. Through an examination of his career, he learned that what he loved most about his job was world travel, and what he was running away from was government bureaucracy and its lack of entrepreneurial opportunities.

I found him a position in import-export sales. He had contacts in the foreign countries where his company did business, knew how their governments worked and what the import-export laws were. The move into sales brought him more money, more satisfaction and the opportunity to maintain and build upon a twenty-year contact base.

An elegant, fashionable woman over sixty had been working for a nonprofit organization, calling on corporations for donations. Despite the fact that she was a top performer, she was poorly paid and got little job satisfaction. We determined she would be ideally suited to the position of outside sales representative for a temporary employment service, calling on the same clients she had contacted as a nonprofit fundraiser. She enjoyed an immediate 20 percent raise in salary plus commission, Fortune 500 benefits she had not enjoyed before, a company car and an expense account. The people she did business with began to view her as a successful business executive, rather than as one of those charity ladies.

"I love my job! I love my job! I love my job! I love my boss! I love my clients! I love this company! And most of all I love my new career in advertising space sales!" wrote Sales Athlete® Roxanne Brown in a delightful letter of gratitude. "After two years of selling video cassettes, covering a territory that ranged from Vermont to Ohio to Georgia to Florida, working seven days a week, twenty-four hours a day, I now have my dream job," she explained. "I'm working a forty-hour work week, no weekends, making more money than I ever dreamed of with promotional opportunities in the offing. I wake up every morning and can't wait to start my day. How strange! After all those years of floundering, I've finally found my niche, thanks to the Sales Athlete®. I am happier than I've ever been and have more energy than I thought possible. What a profound effect one's career has on every facet of one's life!"

When Roxanne joined the Sales Athlete® program, she examined the ten different types of sales careers it targeted and decided that instead of a route sales job, she wanted a business-to-business selling situation. Within that arena, we identified the kind of people she wanted to do business with: designers, architects, contractors. She wanted to access these people through prearranged appointments instead of canvassing by telephone or soliciting them in person without appointments; to sell a higher ticket item; and to have a manager who was willing to train her in a new profession.

After a few short training sessions, Roxanne learned what you will know after reading this book. There is no moment like the moment when you have found your special niche and begin giving it your all. If you train yourself using the Sales Athlete® program, you'll experience that moment, and many more to come as you enjoy the rewards of career satisfaction.

The greatest satisfaction of my own work is to take people lost in mediocrity and walk them through the simple steps to vocational satisfaction, success and security.

It's not that hard to beat a mediocre work life. Sadly, though, not many people achieve the career success they deserve—not because success is hard to achieve, but because they never reached out to anybody who cared enough to get them to stop what they were doing and concentrate fully on the subject of their own success.

I care. Come along with me and take a look at your career options.

The Ten Types of Sales Jobs

To help you choose the right niche, here is a list of the ten basic types of sales jobs, with examples of industries that employ these sales methods and their income-earning potential.

1) Retail Sales

Retail selling involves working in restaurants, weight-control centers and daycare centers—any business where customers walk in off the street and the floor salespeople translate those customers into sales. If you like person-to-person contact with the public, this job can be very psychologically rewarding.

Gail works in the Chanel boutique at Saks Fifth Avenue. She loves the customers she serves, knows their wardrobes and lifestyles, and believes in herself as a fashion consultant. She flourishes in an environment where she can follow trends in design and serve fashionable people who rely upon her taste and advice. For Gail, retail sales is the perfect fit.

Retail jobs start at minimum wage and go up to a maximum of around $36,000 a year.

2) Route Sales

Most route sales do not involve high-ticket items: pharmaceuticals, a case of chewing gum, mineral water, frozen foods, popcorn, chips, pantyhose or soap—anything sold to a drug or grocery store. The job requires that you arrive on the premises of a supermarket, drugstore or warehouse and perform inventory control, frequently writing the orders and checking competitive product placement. These are the kinds of jobs you see in large newspaper ads: "Career opportunity, major corporation, MBA required."

Corporations recruit primarily from college campuses for these jobs, luring young talent with the promise of a fast-track executive training program that begins at the bottom, stocking shelves. These training programs, while based in grocery store aisles and warehousing facilities, are highly regarded and build a fine foundation for a lucrative career in executive business-to-business selling. Most often route sales jobs require a willingness to relocate every few years while on the corporate trail toward that big job at headquarters.

Salaries range from $19,200 to $27,500, with another $500 to $1,500 a year in bonuses, plus a company car and such "golden handcuff" benefits as tuition refunds, paternity/maternity leaves and vision care. Changes in how the IRS taxes these benefits may lead to additional taxes taken out of base pay. You move up this compensation ladder at the rate of 10 percent a year.

3) Showroom Sales

Like retail jobs, these jobs are characterized by people coming to you. Jobs selling furniture and fashion "to the trade" and automobiles to the public fall into this category.

To make a decent living in showroom sales, the salesperson has to have a following, or be willing to produce one through soliciting clients over the telephone and direct mail presentations and inviting them into the showroom. This is a good opportunity if you don't like getting in and out of a car all the time or traveling a territory.

If you decide to pursue showroom sales, we encourage you to develop a loyal clientele because your income and vocational security will be dependent upon your ability to draw people into that showroom and close those sales.

Income in this sales area is a salary of $1,000 to $3,000 per month, plus commissions and overrides, with a total compensation of $16,000 to $60,000 a year. You can expect annual increases of $2,500 to $5,000 per year due to an expanding contact base.

4) In-Your-Own-Business Sales

This is the arena of real estate agents, independent stockbrokers and insurance agents. You run your own business, with the support of a corporate plan and a solid business reputation to back you up.

In some cases, selling in your own business is a smart way to go. But the question to ask yourself is this: Are you an employee or an entrepreneur? Many people seek my counsel because they are unhappy with the pressure they feel in this type of sales work and are failing because they lack an entrepreneurial spirit. Many need to be employees. They want the camaraderie of an office, they want support systems, benefits and guidelines.

If you are thinking of going into your own sales business, you'll need self-discipline and an independent character. Both qualities are required to build a business where all leads are self-generated.

Usually the salary or draw given you by sponsoring organizations is very low—in the $18,000 to $24,000 range—while you go through licensing. After licensing, you roll over into a draw against commissions. In your first year you can expect to earn a little over $30,000, and if you meet "plan," you are expected to increase your compensation by $7,000 to $12,000 a year.

5) New-Business, No-Repeat, Cold-Call, Low-Price Sales

"New-business, no-repeat" selling means that you are generating new leads for your company, and once the leads become actual clients, they are turned over to another representative. "Cold-call" sales require that you arrive on the premises of a prospect without a prearranged appointment. "Low-price" sales involve items such as pencils, as opposed to higher-priced merchandise such as telephone systems.

Rita came to me when the YWCA she'd been staying in told her she'd have to move on to other quarters by the end of the week. She'd already been evicted from her apartment and simply couldn't find a job. I told her to look in the newspaper ads for a position with an office supply company, and find a company that would pay salespeople their first commission checks within a week. She found one, and was given the Beverly Hills territory.

In her first week, she sold $1,000 worth of office supplies and got a check for $250. She stayed on that job long enough to get back on her feet. She made terrific contacts, while also honing skills in accessing, presentation and closing. Today Rita is an account manager with a medical billing service, calling on medical offices and hospitals, earning $40,000 a year.

Another example of this type of sales job: A client asked me to find someone to call on auto body shops part time and represent a revolutionary new paint removal system. The job was not to sell the system, but to travel from one body shop to the next, leaving sales materials. Each cold-call visit earned $1.50, in addition to a $200 base salary.

This type of job generates house accounts for a parent company. Salaries tend to be low, although there are high commissions for first-time customer orders.

Time spent in this area of sales will serve as great training in accessing clients and in rapid establishment of rapport—skills that will shorten the selling cycle when applied to business-to-business executive sales.

6) New-Business, No-Repeat, Telephone-Solicitation, Low-Price Sales

A job working for the telephone company, selling bold listings in the Yellow Pages, falls into this category. The most obvious representation of this type of job is the one characterized in the newspapers: "Earn $60,000 a year" selling travel club memberships, magazine subscriptions or duplicator toner. They are boiler-room operations. However, they are right for some people some of the time—out-of-work actors and actresses, for example, or people on the West Coast who like to work from 6:00 A.M. to 1:00 P.M. telemarketing on the East Coast.

Jobs in this sales category pay quickly and would be worth pursuing if you have a short-term goal in mind: raising extra cash for Christmas or escrow money for your house. The work also helps hone your skills in accessing prospects over the telephone. Overall, this category sometimes represents a good job.

7) New-Business, No-Repeat, High-Price Sales

Jet planes. Large computer systems. Telephone systems. Whole suites of furniture for new offices. These are things people buy only once. Rarely do the sales jobs in these areas go to entry-level people, because the training investment is so substantial.

You can't cold-call an office building asking who wants a jet. Before considering a job in this category take into account the way the organization promotes itself, how it generates leads and the contacts you would bring to the job.

Recently a man with a private pilot's license came to me for counseling to help him identify a profession that would allow him to use his license every day. Because my husband leased planes for the rock bands he manages, I had met a number of sales representatives who leased corporate jets. I referred him to these people, and after his first meeting with one of these contacts, he called me to say he'd been offered a position. It seemed so easy, he said, he was probably going to turn it down and keep looking. "Don't!" I replied.

Opportunities in big-ticket sales that pay salaries plus commissions for inexperienced sales representatives without contacts are rare. This category draws its salespeople largely from those who have worked their way up in the mailroom, are in the family business or bring extensive product knowledge or a mighty contact base to their work.

8) Servicing and Expanding Existing Corporate Accounts

This is the arena of industrial or advertising agency account executives, insurance company representatives to independent agents, of General Motors dealer representatives and Hertz Rent-a-Car representatives who call on corporations to sign them up for frequent rental discounts.

This executive route sales job can be performed over the telephone or in person. Rarely are you expected to do more than enhance an existing account. Your job is to make sure the client/customer is happy and troubleshoot any problems that come up in the account. As the contract comes up for renewal, you and your manager will frequently present an annual overview of any planned changes in prices, rates or fees. Many of my own industrial accounts have positions such as these to service their wholesale distributor networks and major accounts.

Compensation is usually comfortable—in the 30's to high 70's, usually with high quotas based on the previous year's sales and small commissions paid over and above annual projections. The range here is very broad, from year-end bonuses of a few hundred dollars to sums equal to one and—yes—two times the annual base pay.

9) Products You Manufacture, Warehouse, Distribute and Endorse

This can involve your secret recipe for liver paté, which you sell to restaurant pantries, or the quilts you make in your basement and sell to country stores. It is labor intensive—therefore you are limited first of all by the number of hours in the day.

It is very common for people to contact my service having had this type of selling experience. They were undercapitalized, unable to meet the demand for their product. These are writers, executive producers of film projects, managers of Mrs. Fields cookie outlets. Success in this category requires both an entrepreneurial spirit and a good mind for detail.

The question to ask yourself is this: How involved with the total project do you want to be? Do you want 100 percent control of manufacturing, administration and selling, or control of only one of those areas? If you want control of all of these aspects, you should have some talent and training in manufacturing, warehousing, distribution and administration. Cottage industries are vulnerable when inadequate research has been done in any of these areas. It is easy to lose control when the products you manufacture start piling up in every room of your house or office or when orders come in faster than they can possibly be filled.

Earnings in this category range from "pin money" to millions of dollars—depending upon your product, organization and skill in business and sales.

One woman built a $40 million business from her home computer by designing a piece of software that has revolutionized the fashion inventory business. With her program, buyers can plug into a computer the price, fabric and design details they want from a manufacturer, and manufacturers can design their lines to fit buyers' specifications.

10) Executive Business-To-Business Repeat Sales

The emphasis of the Sales Athlete® program is to train you for executive business-to-business selling.

This arena is characterized by a slow start, as the sales athlete develops loyalty with clients who are currently doing business with competitive companies.

The biggest obstacle he or she must overcome is a company's satisfaction with its existing resource. Business-to-business sales are frequently contracted, and renewable annually. The arena includes sales of industrial products, printing services, advertising space, banking services, computer software, packaging, recycling and waste management services. It also includes executive recruitment services and franchise relations, in which you sell both franchises and the products and marketing services used by franchised companies.

Since you can take your contacts from one year to the next, the commissions build from year to year. When you move up, you move up in tall steps. You may start at $24,000 a year, but then build your income at a rate of $1,000 a month.

Defining Your Ideal Sales Job

Take a good look at the list of ten sales categories just discussed. Eliminate those that you know won't fit your lifestyle or career plan. Zero in on your ideal job. Finally, think about how your ideal job would work out on the basis of the criteria we discussed at the beginning of this chapter:

1) What kinds of people would you like to communicate with in the course of your day-to-day assignment? Purchasing agents? Sales managers? Company presidents? Financial managers? Blue-collar company managers? Bankers?

2) How would you like to reach these people? Over the telephone, followed by in-person, prearranged appointments? Cold-calling in office buildings? Closing on furnished leads? By letter?

3) How complex or simple would you like your day-to-day assignment to be? This question is best answered by looking at the realities of your personal life. Do you have small children, for example, who require a great deal of your mental energy? If so, perhaps you'd be better off with assignments that in-

volve only a few relatively simple steps. If your personal life is unencumbered, you might eagerly embrace the opportunity to tackle more complex projects from beginning to end. This is a *lifestyle* decision. Keep in mind too that the complexity or simplicity of a chosen assignment has *no* effect whatsoever on the amount of money you'll be able to earn.

4) What managerial or corporate style suits you best? Do you see yourself in a conservative, buttoned-down, old-guard firm, representing its traditional style as well as its product or service? Do you want to walk into an office that hustles and bustles with electric tension, or would you prefer something more laid-back and contemplative?

Once you have an idea of what your ideal job profile would look like, you are ready to conduct a job-search survey of employers. Your search will be far more comprehensive—and a lot more fun—than the usual demoralizing prospect of perusing newspaper classified ads and sending out resumés to faceless employers. It starts with identifying an industry or industries you think might provide you with the opportunities and lifestyle you want.

Let's say you have chosen to explore the field of hazardous waste removal. The need for top-quality firms in this area is growing, exciting new technologies are being developed in the field and you feel confident you could represent these services. What next?

Pick up the Yellow Pages and find "Hazardous Waste Removal Services." List all of the companies within your geographical area. Then begin an over-the-telephone survey of every company on your list. Ask to speak to anybody on the sales staff.

When a sales representative answers and identifies himself by name, write down the name. Politely explain that you are in the middle of an in-depth career search that requires you to speak to someone who is performing the job you ideally want to perform. Punctuate your statement with: "Would you be kind enough to answer five questions? It will only take a minute."

Expect a pause, while the rep assesses whether it is worth his time. Most likely, he'll place a value on his time and say, "I only have a minute—shoot."

First ask for the exact titles of the people on the company's sales staff and write them down: "sales representative" or "account representative," for example. Should you decide to apply to this company in the future, use the appropriate title as your career objective—it improves your chances of your application being reviewed by the hiring manager. The less scrutiny your application receives by the hiring manager's secretary, the better your chances are of getting an interview.

Your second question should be: "By title, who are your key client prospects? That is, who do you do business with on a day-to-day basis?" Write down his answers. This will tell you who you would be required to communicate with regularly, whether company presidents or purchasing agents.

Next question: "How do you gain access to these people?" Again, write down the answers: Telephone solicitation, cold-calling in person, prearranged appointments, furnished leads.

Fourth question: "Once you gain access to these prospects, what steps do you take to complete your projects?" He might reply: "We assess the company's needs, then present our company, request an opportunity to demonstrate appropriate products, negotiate all the details, monitor delivery and then maintain contact for reorders." Jot this down.

Your last question: "What kinds of people does your company hire in sales?" He might say, "We only hire people with a B.S. in chemistry" or "Well, we've got an ex-waiter from the restaurant where the sales manager has lunch everyday . . ." (Ah! This reveals that the company has a flexible hiring profile.)

All this may seem intimidating, but remember—most sales people are happy to help people starting out. After all, you might end up as a buyer, a manager or peer one day. Thousands of people who have taken my seminars have found great success with just such career surveys. They are amazed at the number of people who are so generous with their time.

Use a separate sheet of paper for each company you call, and run through the same five questions with a salesperson from each company in the industry you have chosen to survey. Even if you have fifty companies to call, this should take no more than a day or two. And what do you have when you're through? You have an overview of the industry you're interested in. You will end up with a good idea about the style of salespeople within that industry and the differences in the companies. You will have a realistic idea of what kinds of people these companies hire, and you will be better qualified to assess whether or not the industry suits you.

Most importantly perhaps, you will have made a contact within each of the companies you have chosen to explore—that list of people who so kindly took time to answer your questions.

The "Touchdown" Strategy for Accessing a New Career

The first contact with a prospective employer is over the telephone with a sales representative.

The next contact is a thank-you note to each person who helped complete your survey. "Thank you so much for helping me with the hardest part of getting started."

The third contact, ideally, takes place at an industry function attended by representatives of the companies you have surveyed. You might find out, for example, the date and location of the Regional Hazardous Waste Haulers Association meeting. Before the meeting, transfer the names you collected from your phone survey to an index card. On one side of the card, list the names of the representatives in alphabetical order, followed by the name of the company each person represents. Flip the card over and list the company names alphabetically, then the name of their representative.

Now, off to the function. Of course, you don't know a soul. Not a soul. Don't panic: You are armed with the index card listing the names of all your contacts. (You've also brought along copies of your resumé, but more about that later.)

You spot someone with a nametag—"Beth Hughes, WasteCo." You haven't spoken to Beth before, but on your card is the name of Matt Moore, your contact at WasteCo.

You approach Beth and say, "Beth, I see you're with WasteCo. I spoke to Matt Moore on your sales staff a while back, and he's the reason I'm here tonight. I've decided that I really want to pursue a career in waste management service sales. Is Matt here tonight?"

Your opening remark is so confident that it inspires Beth to have confidence in you. She may even say something like, "I don't see Matt, but let me introduce you to Suzanne Deal over here who has a job bank." Your networking begins.

If someone asks you in the course of the meeting, "What is that card?" you would state the following: "I just completed an in-depth career search program and decided that what I wanted to do next is pursue a career in sales. The program outlined twenty industries and I discounted nineteen, since I really want to focus only on waste management. Everyone I spoke to is listed on this card. And where I'd first just thought I wanted to pursue a career in this industry, after meeting and seeing everyone here, now I *know* this is the field for me."

At this pont, you've designated yourself as a low-risk hire. Your determined pursuit of a career will be impressive. Most people just do not do this sort of thing: They look at ads in the newspapers, or an upstairs neighbor says, "Why don't you pursue . . . ?" You've used a system that puts you in the right place *all the time,* and *you* are picking and choosing your arena.

Another way to dazzle people from an industry you've targeted is one that might cause goose bumps, but it's sure to win you points for courage. When everyone is seated at the industry meeting, and you are asked to introduce yourself, boldly stand up and announce: "I've just undertaken an in-depth career search, and have decided that this is the industry I want to pursue. So if any of you knows of a company that might be looking for someone like me, please take a copy of my resumé—I've left them on the table in the back."

Do you know what the response will be? Applause!

That spectacular third contact smoothly paves your way to your fourth contact: follow-up notes or telephone calls to people you've met at the meeting.

The fifth contact is the job interview.

Before any interview, and before submitting a resumé to any company with a specific opening, the sales athlete targets the resumé to the job, using the information gathered about the company and the sales position from the five-question phone survey.

The resumé will pull from your experience those jobs and situations in which you have proven you can access people the company would want you to access by means they would have you use (cold-call, telephone or letter), it will demonstrate that you can complete the type of day-to-day assignment required for the job and that you fit the profile and management style of the company.

In the actual interview, you repeat that experience. The most difficult moment in a job interview can be when a prospective employer says, "We're really looking for someone with five years of experience in this particular area," and you have only one or none at all. You can't stop interviewers from saying that, but you *can* turn the remark into a sales aid.

You can say, "Mr. Smith, I know you're now trying to evaluate the best possible talent in terms of the ability to communicate with those people you're required to communicate with, someone who can access these people, someone who can see an assignment through from beginning to end, someone who will do well within your corporate culture. *Please* look at my resumé, and what you will see is that in each and every one of my assignments, I have been required to communicate with this echelon of executive and I *have* accessed these people. In fact, though it doesn't yet add up to five years, I have a track record in accessing, presenting and negotiating details, and in maintaining contact to make sure accounts are being handled extremely well."

Dress for the interview like the people in the targeted company dress, and point out that you fit the profile of the company. You might mention that you have spoken to some of the company's salespeople and are confident you would fit in well with the staff. Point out similarities between yourself and the company's top sales producer. You might add, "I do my best work under conditions like these," and describe the atmosphere of the company in positive terms.

Don't forget to let your prospective employer know you are a hard worker. Most sales jobs are not nine-to-five jobs. Many people go into sales jobs, in fact, because the hours are flexible. Most employers, however, want somebody who is willing to put in a forty-hour week, from nine to five. Stress that you are, and that you can be flexible with your hours according to the company's needs.

When you've completed your interview, follow it up with a note: "As I was driving back to the office after our interview, I took the opportunity to review everything we discussed. . . ."

You may have wondered by now why I haven't mentioned the newspaper classified ads—the traditional hunting ground of job-seekers—as a good place to look for a job. Don't discount them, but don't count on them either. They shouldn't be your only resource. Nevertheless, if you see an ad for a job that seems interesting, pick up the telephone, ask for someone in sales at that company and conduct the same telemarketing survey outlined above. If the job seems to fit your goals and the person asks whether you are calling specifically about the ad, you can respond, "This sounds like a great job—you mean to say there's an *opening?*"

While I caution you against relying solely on general newspaper classified ads, I implore you to use the classified sections of trade newspapers and industry magazines. These advertisements will tell you in far more detail about a job—and your savvy in scouting the industry's own media will be appreciated by prospective employers.

A sales athlete never stops looking for a great job. We live in an era of deregulation, mergers and rapidly changing technologies, and most of us will need to work far into the future. Through no fault of your own, tomorrow could be your last in the job you now enjoy. Don't end up on the bench.

CHAPTER 3

The Performance Strategy of a Sales Athlete

Every year, thousands of people looking for added satisfaction from their executive sales careers come to me with problems that seem to them insurmountable.

In auditoriums and corporate conference rooms, they raise their hands or pull me aside, confiding:

"I can't find the time in my crazy schedule to fit in my personal life, let alone an exercise program."

"My territory is too small and I can't seem to expand it."

"My territory is too large and I can't seem to control it."

"I've hit $600,000 with my account base, but I

can't get beyond that. I need to reach a million to make projection. I'm overwhelmed by quotas and the management requirement to make a specified number of sales calls every day."

"Maybe a career in executive sales is not for me. I can't imagine doing anything else, but my job just isn't working out."

"I'm financially successful at last, but my life is so stressful I don't know whether it's worth it. I'm tired all the time."

All of these problems and many more are easily solved. No matter how complex the problems are, when tackled with the performance strategy offered by the Sales Athlete® training program they are soon gone. Every area you have identified in the skills test in Chapter 1 also can be helped by using a simple, three-point performance strategy.

I have developed a strategy that is simple, sophisticated and effective in addressing blocks that are keeping you from achieving your goals. If you follow it, you will be able to break down and tackle problems before they become career injuries.

A Three-Tier Performance Strategy for Prioritizing Your Actions, Targeting Associations and Moving Past Fear and Self-Doubt

Are you afraid you'll wind up like the retired seventy-year-old professional who came into my office frustrated because she couldn't find a job, "even in a five-and-dime"?

You should be. According to U.S. Department of Health, Education and Welfare statistics, a mere three percent of us are able to support ourselves past age sixty-five without government or family assistance.

Ultimately, if at age sixty-five you have to work or want to work, the assets that you will draw upon will be those that you developed during your most productive working years. So *right now,* focus on getting 100 percent out of your career. Follow the three-tier strategy outlined here and see how sales athletes beat the odds.

1) A Sales Athlete Prioritizes Activity

Before your stomach clenches at the thought of running yourself into the ground for the next ten or fifteen years, relax.

Leave behind the idea of "controlling" time, and in its place begin to think "prioritizing." You may have read books exhorting you to "get in control," and after following all the steps carefully realized that something always comes up and makes your plans go awry—leaving you once again "out of control." It becomes a vicious circle as you see yourself failing to stay on top of things.

Sales athletes are successful in fields ranging from creative writing to selling commercial accounts for banks and all of them lead full and busy lives. Yet their appearance is never harried; they never give you the sense they would rather be or should be somewhere else. How do they manage?

"I can't believe you—working seven days a week!" a friend tells me. My answer to that is, "It may look that way because I'm giving a barbecue for clients at 2:00 on Sunday afternoon—but that's not really work; that's fun. And at 7:00 every Tuesday evening, I get a massage—that's not work; that's rest." My work is fun because I prioritize time according to "high leverage" goals and objectives. The Sales Athlete® program breaks down activity into eight projects: mental and physical health, family, financial well-being, prospecting new business, seeing these new contacts through to the signing of the contract and serving existing business. That's actually six; I leave two project areas flexible and ready for opportunity. I prioritize by using the principle of eight projects integrated into a seven-day week.

Wouldn't you rather live that way—enjoying your business associates enough to spend time with them *off* the job, and still having purely personal time to pamper yourself on a regular basis?

For years, people have gone into sales and marketing careers because these careers offer flexibility and independence not usually found in other businesses. But that built-in flexibility doesn't mean you automatically have the tools to use your time 100 percent effectively, as all the salespeople overwhelmed with lists of details will attest.

Sales athletes prepare both for the sprint through today and the eighteen-month marathon required to complete a major project. To plan that way, you need to recognize that each day, each month, is made up of thousands of details—and that you must take charge of them, instead of letting details consume your time and mental energy insidiously.

After experimenting with several self-management systems, I was fortunate enough to be retained as a consultant and sales trainer for Time/Design, a company that literally has time management down to a science. I was contracted to train their temporary sales force. These representatives were to explain the system and any changes to new and existing customers over the telephone between October and January, the peak Time/Design ordering period.

As part of my research for this training, I was introduced to over thirty popular time management systems. I examined each closely in order to answer the comparative questions of the most skeptical prospects.

I coupled this research with a questionnaire I handed out and collected from the open enrollment Sales Athlete® sales trainings I was presenting nationally.

Not only was my own experience in adapting this system to the performance strategy of the Sales Athlete® program easy, but hundreds of sales athletes recommended the Time/Design system for the exact same reasons.

I believe the Time/Design self-management

system is easy to integrate into your personal and professional life because it sets up a natural flow of information, planning and *action* that carries you through a project's detailed activities in a clear and comprehensive manner consistent with the Sales Athlete® performance strategy. The system organizes time by hourly, daily, monthly and annual segments, and integrates management of up to ten projects into each time frame.

If your time management system helps you keep on top of both your time and your activities—right now and into next year—you'll discover you *can* keep your personal and professional life in balance. You'll start meeting deadlines and remembering crucial dates. Most importantly, you'll enjoy an overview of your time that will help you continually set and adjust priorities.

"There is no such thing as time management," says Peter Vedro, director of training and development for Time/Design. "You can only manage yourself."

The goal of a time management system is to show you clearly where you are going, why you are going there, what you expect to get when you arrive and what materials you need to accomplish your goals.

People who use a management system are very

effective; they focus on high-leverage, high-priority actions and therefore are never very "busy." "They're self-managed, self-directed, self-motivated, self-productive.

The ideal time management system allows you to gain that all-important overview of your life and your goals by simply giving you one place in which to jot down all your priorities. With a system that lets you map out short- and long-term career goals and integrate them with your personal life, you'll fall prey to fewer crises.

The system allows you to continually shift emphasis and priorities as opportunities present themselves. The sales athlete looks never to miss an opportunity. Sales athletes are always "in the right place at the right time" because they have planned to be there. Associates call them lucky, but in fact they simply have learned to prioritize their time.

One day, shortly after I had started using Time/Design in my own life, I managed to overcommit myself by forty-eight hours in a single day. Had I tried to do all I'd told myself I could do that day, I would have given short shrift to everything on my agenda and ended the day feeling harried, incomplete—a member of that ignominious society of people enmeshed in "superior mediocrity."

My management system bailed me out by making clear what my high-leverage choices and priorities were, those that gave me the most significant return on my investment of time and energy.

I *had* to tend to the administrative chore of closing out the month and producing projections for the next quarter. I could reschedule writing the address for a program ten days later. Once I'd cleared my schedule my mind was completely free to focus effectively on the present. The address I'd rescheduled to write turned out to be one of my best, because it was written without annoying distractions and pressures from conflicting obligations.

Having an overview of my time freed me from the stresses of overcommitment and imbalance, turning me into a "100 percenter." It was the moment I met myself at my creative, problem-solving best and fell in love with my new time management system.

I use it to plan in detail the next two weeks, to map out more broadly the month and year ahead and to manage up to eight projects (writing this book was one of them) at one time, including lecturing and servicing of clients.

Every time I have a new idea, I jot it down in the appropriate file in my databank, which keeps track of client birthdays and marriages, as well as informing me of account profitability. My system has a section for family matters, new business development, current accounts and floating projects (including household matters, car maintenance and the planning of social events).

On each daily page I list planned activities and prioritize them from A to C. If an emergency or unexpected "priority A" event occurs, I can quickly move a "C" activity to another day or time slot, so it never falls through the cracks. You might have noted the comfort and relief you feel when you walk into your office, pick up a pile of messages, organize them according to priorities—A, B or C. As you return the calls, a C call may become an A call, an A may become a B. What I love about my Time/Design is that it allows me to prioritize that way with everything in my life—from time with my husband to training programs that may take weeks to develop.

I recently planned a tenth-year celebration of business in Los Angeles. The entertainment included Samoan dancers, fireworks, exploding feathers, a cake in the form of the Pacific Basin complete with a smoldering volcano, a blizzard of bubbles, showers of orchids and a toast using special port from a prized port collection, a gift from one of my most satisfied clients.

Some people would never conceive of such an

elaborate event; not because they lack creativity, but because they "just don't have the time."

While I was making all these plans, I learned that a group of Western European businessmen would be in California to inspect their U.S. operation. I had done some consulting work developing their sales materials for the U.S. market. Their product was great and their sales brochure beautiful—the best I had ever seen—but their salespeople needed training. They were not getting to the right decisionmakers and didn't know how to negotiate with Americans—they needed the Sales Athlete® sales training.

The committee of decision-makers for this company would be in Los Angeles on a tight schedule. I wanted to plan an event that would welcome an outsider into their management meeting. My own schedule was tight. I was on a time budget, but recognized the urgent necessity of reaching these people and building this important account into a satisfied sales training client.

I selected a French Caribbean restaurant with a bistro setting—a European touch. I thought the group would feel at home there.

On a weekend break, I personally visited the restaurant and preplanned four appetizer-portion courses with the chef, with vegetarian options. I was attentive to the smallest details: These men would be on Paris time, and planning a heavy meal would have been insensitive to their physical clocks. I had a calligrapher design an invitation, outlining the time, date and menu. The invitation was then duplicated and hand-delivered with a basket of wafers, fruits, cheeses and breads for their morning coffee break.

All seven of the prospects RSVP'd that they would be delighted to attend the dinner. The restaurant set up a round table for easy conversation. Two days later we signed a healthy five-figure contract before their return to Europe. And—it took less time to plan the dinner than it would have taken me to drive back and forth across town to their offices in the middle of the day.

For two weeks, I was organizing those two events simultaneously. Both were part of my seventh project. Yet I *still* had room in my management system to take on an eighth project as opportunities presented themselves. At all times I was aware I had the ability to successfully take on and complete one more project. The priority was to value the opportunity of "one more project."

A management system doesn't add more time to your day, but it does free you from unrealistic expectations of what can be done with the time that's available. It helps you balance priorities and take care of details that might otherwise be put off to the crisis point. Being super-organized is not, as you might expect, a tyranny. Disorganization is. Prioritizing frees you to work and live your creative best, because the real you, the creative you, can be found on that clean surface underneath the pile of distracting details on your desk. Sales athletes put all of the details in their place, easy to retrieve on demand. They are free to initiate new ideas and projects and are able to focus 100 percent of their creative problem-solving strength on each well-organized project.

Finding time to do what you say you will do is a key to building client loyalty. Again and again you'll hear variations of this: "I can't believe that as busy as you are, you still found time to . . ." Each time it will be the voice of a satisfied recipient.

2) A Sales Athlete Targets Associations

Stop looking at your *job* as the source of financial security. It's not. Jobs come and go as companies merge, the economy shifts, markets and technologies advance. Having a secure future means setting priorities and targeting your associations.

I suggest you begin with the exercise of transferring names into a new address book. What you will have is an overview of your contacts—but that's not as important as the names themselves. Take a good look at those names. What you are looking at is your *career equity*.

Through years of counseling experienced and inexperienced salespeople I've grown to believe that it's not what you know but who knows what you know that determines your vocational security.

The strategy of targeting associations can ensure your security straight through to retirement. Even the best of jobs provides *no* security unless it is combined with proper attention to contacts, as my client Linda learned.

Twenty years ago, Linda was the secretary to a man who bought all the rights to black-and-white TV classics. Linda's job was to sell these shows to local television stations. Working most days from 7:00 A.M. to 7:00 P.M., she built her account base into a $25-million territory. She was promoted to vice president of marketing, and built her own salary up to over $100,000 a year. Content to work hard at her job, after a long day at her office she would opt for a solitary walk on the beach instead of attending key association meetings or social functions within her industry.

When her company was suddenly sold, Linda was replaced by a nephew of the new owner, who gave her a seemingly generous year's salary as severance pay. Linda spent the next year on vacation, doing nothing to gain access to another job.

Six months after her year's vacation ended, Linda's car was repossessed, she was about to lose her home, and her confidence had eroded to the point that she could barely speak audibly.

She retained my counseling services. I quickly assessed her track record and contact base and took her to the next industry association meeting in her field. I found that the results of her career were well-known, but no one knew of Linda herself. She never recognized the wisdom of that adage: It's not what you know but who knows what you know that determines your vocational security.

We need to assess clients and associates in terms of future or long-range potential. The most valuable contacts are those that we could take with us from job to job.

All good sales representatives know they must implement the marketing plan for their product. Sales athletes learn how to develop marketing plans for *themselves*.

After you have spent six months on a new job, you may want to perform a "sales physical." Frequently, people new to jobs are so involved with day-to-day selling and the problems of meeting quotas that they are unable to distinguish between the goals set by sales managers and the goals they must set to protect their own future.

My job is to bring sales executives up into a "tower" so they can look down at all of their prospects and identify the most profitable ones. Those are the prospects who will remain good clients indefinitely and continue to buoy the sales athlete's career.

Years later when I see sales athletes again, they may be in different jobs, but those valuable, targeted associations will have remained with them as contacts and clients.

One sales athlete I know targeted his associations early in the game and came up with this winning strategy: Matt had started his career by selling duplicators in the 1960s. In the '70s, the price and commission in duplicators dropped, but top executives and forward-thinking families were beginning to buy desktop computers. Using insights gained from his contacts, Matt was able to assess, with little risk, the need his clients had for desktop PCs. He moved into this high-commission field, selling personal computers to the same clients who had previously purchased duplicating machines from him. Those clients liked him and, because of the consistency of his services, they believed in this new application of technology for their homes and offices.

By 1982, if Matt had stayed with computers, he would have had to work twice as hard—doubling or tripling his client base—in order to make what he earned two years earlier. Instead, he began successfully selling data communications equipment and services to his contacts. By this time many of Matt's clients had been doing business with him for over twenty years. Matt actively cared for his clients, and they remained loyal to him. Over the years, they steadily added referrals to his client base.

Matt was consistently sensitive to competition in the market and among his peers. He built a strong defense that buoyed him from one step to the next in his career. That's how he increased his income each year and assured himself of a financially secure retirement.

Linda, on the contrary, ignored the fact that she was in a competitive industry. Secure in her job, she didn't see a need to develop a strong defensive position within her field. Rather than laying a solid foundation by building career equity with her contacts, she chose to believe that her job was enough to provide career security.

When I started working with Linda she was close to ruin. As I began to take her to industry functions I watched her self-confidence blossom as people complimented her on her past work. By becoming visible at these functions, she made it clear she was available for employment. Linda was quickly snatched up to syndicate a new exercise show to independent television stations.

This is not to suggest that just so long as you're a nice person with a ready smile and a hefty Rolodex your acquaintances can be transformed into loyal business contacts eager to support you in your declining years. Strategic planning with your contact base is critical to your career. If you are insensitive to it you'll end up like Linda before her comeback—isolated, and with depleted self-confidence. If you recognize its importance you'll have vocational and income security as long as you live.

3) A Sales Athlete Moves Past Fear and Self-Doubt

I was a seven-year-old Camp Fire Girl when I first learned that moving past fear could bring me success in sales. We lived in a tiny rural community, and when it came time for the annual candy sale, prospects were slim indeed.

By the time I made my rounds, the few merchants in the area had already bought boxes of candy from their next-door neighbors, granddaughters or nieces. Most of the Camp Fire Girls sold their quota to their own parents. My parents, however, were not financially able to buy my few cases of chocolate almond bars. That left me with two choices: suffer the humiliation of returning the unsold cases, or approach the one remaining prospect in town—the neighborhood "monster."

Sadly, this man who was feared by the local children was reclusive because he had suffered serious, disfiguring burns over most of his body. He lived in a ramshackle house, and since we never saw him, in our small imaginations he had become a terrifying person.

I knocked on his door, fully prepared to race

away should he scream at me or attack me with a knife. Instead, he was so pleased that I had come to visit him, he bought all of my candy bars. I befriended him and he became my loyal customer.

As an adult, I've had other "monsters" to face: a fear of public speaking and the fear of repeated rejection. Over the years, I've developed an urgent need to remove anxiety and move past these fears, because fear wastes time. No moment is as satisfying as when I emerge victorious over my own fear.

As gregarious as I appear, I experience anxiety every time I must make a speech before a large group of people. But I've trained myself to get past that anxiety and onto the stage. I've learned to expect a certain amount of inner tension, and to use that energy to propel me forward.

In the early 1970s, David King, the father of the women in the sales movement and president of Careers for Women, Inc. in New York, gave me good counsel on dealing with situations that produce fear: "Just do the best you can, and don't worry about it. If you worry about results, it will hurt your performance. If you concentrate on performing as well as you can, the results will take care of themselves."

The most common fears of salespeople involve public speaking, cold-calling or accessing new prospects, dealing with intimidating people, closing sales, writing business letters and time management. Expertise in these areas comes from the experience of doing, self-confidence from doing them well. Sales athletes get past anxiety by preparing thoroughly, then going ahead and doing what needs to be done. If you remain frozen in a state of anxiety, not only do you deprive yourself of victory, but you will lower your self-esteem in the process.

Think of yourself diving into a cold, clean swimming pool, and how much easier and more exhilarating it is to simply dive in than to inch in, shivering.

Everyone has his own security blanket. What works for you is what's right for you. I use mental rehearsals as a security blanket, as do many others. Here's how it works.

Say you are intimidated about meeting the president of a large company. Take yourself through this rehearsal exercise one step at a time.

Sit back and imagine yourself picking up the telephone, speaking to the secretary, handling whatever hurdles she may present. You are put through to the president. Spend a moment with the president and establish an appointment.

Now visualize yourself packing your briefcase

with materials for your presentation—a good pen for signing the contract, calling cards, brochures, credit applications, every necessity neatly arranged and ready to retrieve on demand.

See yourself enter the building. Now into the elevator and out of the elevator to the receptionist. Introduce yourself and state the purpose of your visit.

You are ushered into the president's office. Shake hands with the prospect for the first time, take a seat, engage in conversation. Your presentation progresses gradually. You request a commitment for the next meeting to pin down details. Then stand, shake hands, engage in warm eye contact.

Finally, exit the office, confident you have established your goals.

As you take yourself through this mental rehearsal, relax by taking deep breaths between each step. If any step along the way causes you to feel anxious, relax and wait a few seconds, then start again at the beginning until you are able to overcome that emotional hurdle.

If you fear public speaking, your self-training could include toastmasters meetings. If it is in-person cold-call canvassing, try role-playing with other salespeople or visualizations like the one above. If it's a fear of closing, rehearse the worst-case scenarios, work through imaginary closes with a peer or manager and move past that fear.

Whatever fear that may be hindering your personal or professional success can be handled if you break it down into these manageable segments. Instead of dreading the task, challenge it head-on: "I'm not going to waste any more time worrying about this." Don't sabotage yourself by waiting until you *must* face a fear-filled challenge to begin training yourself.

Years ago, I went to hear Mary Wells Lawrence speak, and was taken by the fact that she didn't use a lectern or a microphone to address our large group. At the end of her address, I asked her at what point she was able to speak without a lectern. She told me, "I am a painfully shy person, but I realized I couldn't let my fear get between my audience and what I have to say." She forced herself to move past her fear in order to connect with her audience and deliver her message.

Long ago I had to leave behind my own fears of speaking without the crutch of a lectern to hide behind. Today, I deliver seven to ten addresses each week, often in unfamiliar auditoriums and conference rooms.

The ability to move through fear is anchored in product knowledge. Unless you firmly believe in the product, service or idea you represent, self-doubt will set in. And unless you believe in your own abilities you will begin to believe the objections you are there to overcome.

If you believe in what you are representing and still experience fear in your day-to-day assignment, it's time to seek out help quickly to remove your self-doubt. The longer self-doubt lingers, the more time you waste—and the more it erodes your self-confidence.

Dr. Roger Russie, a Los Angeles psychologist who specializes in removing blocks to success in sales careers, says many sales professionals may suffer career setbacks when they experience rejection of a sale as a personal rebuff.

"People have natural defenses against anything that makes them feel uncomfortable, so they'll start limiting themselves," Russie says.

"Sales is the *only* career in which you can strike out four out of five times up at bat, end up with a 20 percent closing ratio and win," says Marty Weiner, the number one sales manager in the top-selling regional sales office for Glen Ivy, a resort time-sharing company.

If you have chosen the right arena for your sales/marketing career, the only thing that can stop you from succeeding with those odds is your own self-doubt. If you experience rejections personally, you will damage your self-esteem.

Moving past fear and self-doubt are the third tier of the Sales Athlete® performance strategy, since they are the blocks that stop us in our tracks most often.

A sales athlete seeks out whatever resources necessary to achieve the healthy, "no problem" attitude enjoyed by sales athlete Merrill Brown.

In his early career, when faced with a new territory and cold-calling hundreds of prospects, Brown says he would ask himself, "What's the worst possible thing that can happen? Is someone going to shoot me?" It puts things in perspective.

Improve *your* performance by evaluating your current performance against these three strategies: Are you prioritizing your time, targeting associations and moving past fear? The steps you take will increase your career satisfaction immediately, and lead you to greater success and security.

PART III

Career Success

HOW TO SELL

CHAPTER 4

The "Touchdown" Strategy

The original sales athlete, O.B. Bond, taught me how our income in sales is based upon our ability to handle the fear of rejection.

"Your compensation is predicated on the number of no's you will potentially hear," Bond said. "If you were to give away perfume samples at Bloomingdale's at the foot of the escalator, you'd be paid maybe $25,000, and face virtually no rejection. If you are an outside sales representative for the same perfume company, responsible for negotiating shelf space in stores, your compensation would double."

When people come to me and ask how they can make a lot of money quickly, I mentally sort through sales opportunities that have high presentation to closing ratios. In other words, the more potential turndowns a representative must sift through in order to identify and close a sale the more money potentially that representative will earn. Most compensation plans are based on the principle of sweetening the financial incentive so when a representative divides the number of contacts into the final commission to be earned the result is a handsome return for the effort.

Look at the forklift industry. Forklifts went down in price from $45,000 to $12,000 a while back. Not only did the price dive, but the new forklifts are smaller, fit in a truck and help drivers make more deliveries while sustaining fewer delays. Some salespeople in this industry believe it is no longer a lucrative career. It used to be that you'd make fifty calls, sell ten forklifts and earn $1,500 a week. Now, you have to make one hundred fifty calls in order to sell ten and earn the *same* income—about $60,000 to $70,000 per year. People without a history in the industry are able to see the value in this career. Experienced sales representatives in the forklift industry concede it was easier in years past, but recognize that with a little extra effort, they can continue earning more than is possible to earn in many other industries. Sales athletes replace the grumblers who remained inflexible as the industry changed.

In order to have a sales athlete's attitude, you have to deal with the rejection in a professional manner. A sales athlete looks at prospecting as sifting the sands for a gold nugget. Meeting as many people as possible to find the ones who need their products, services and ideas is a maturing, enriching process.

Keep in mind that once you walk into a door to access a prospect, you have a responsibility: You can no longer think of your fear, but of the reverse pyramid method of account service. All of your energy must be spent on discerning and meeting your prospective client's needs, whether the person behind the door is a raging, snarling pit bull or an interested, friendly prospect eager to be sold.

This is the reverse pyramid method of account service: Imagine an inverted pyramid where the client's needs are at the top, your own needs in servicing your client are just below that and your company's needs are at the bottom. It is not a new concept but, sad to say, the method of consistently putting clients' needs first is so rarely used that those who do use it have a strong lead over their competitors.

Frequently, I meet salespeople who concentrate all of their energies on accessing just one or two promising prospects. When deals with both prospects fall through, these people are devastated—and broke. Rather than face early rejection by approaching dozens of prospects, they limit themselves to seemingly sure bets, placing their career security at risk.

Avoid the highs and lows of sales production and the resulting financial bind by developing creative ways to buffer yourself from feeling the rejection personally.

Sales athletes never enjoy or get used to rejection; they become professional "bufferers." They continually add to their sales equipment both verbal and premium buffers—what you might call emotional shinguards that help establish rapport and lower resistance with support personnel and the key decision-maker.

Here is how to apply buffers in serving your clients, shortening your selling cycle and closing sales.

Verbal Buffers

Expect an average of five "touches" with a prospect in order to make a sale. Making those five touches will require creative and strategic planning. In some cases the five touches can take place at one event.

Susan has a temporary employment service specializing in placement in the electronics field. She wants to take advantage of industry events to establish contacts with prospective clients. The next trade show is in New York. Susan gets a copy of the trade show directory, which lists participants.

Her first "touch" is to send out notes to her targeted prospects, saying, "I understand everyone will be meeting after the awards ceremony for drinks and good music at Bice—hope to see you there."

Susan attends the trade show (touch two), and as she is canvassing the aisles, she "buffers" herself by inviting people to talk after the awards ceremony, at Bice, a lively bistro around the corner from the hotel.

After the awards program, many of her prospects indeed drop by the restaurant and Susan meets them there informally (touch three).

After the trade show itself, she will send these prospects brochures that illustrate how her service works (touch four).

Finally, she will call to arrange an appointment to discuss the specifics of how each electronics manufacturer would benefit from her service, and close the sale (touch five).

Susan's strategy is a lot more creative—and buffers her more—than cold-calling trade show booths and hoping for a receptive response on the first approach.

Not only has she taken advantage of the trade show to learn more about the industry she serves and to meet prospects on an informal basis, she has allowed them to meet her and begin to bond with her.

Susan has also used the invitations to buffer herself from the thing she hates most about trade shows—going up to booths where people are doing business and intruding on them with her own proposals. She knows that strategy leads toward rejection and away from sales. Instead, she simply says, "I understand everyone is going down to Bice after dinner." And the prospect responds, "See you then, Susan."

Sales athletes like Susan make a habit of collecting verbal and premium buffers that serve to separate them from all other salespeople, protect themselves from outright rejection and provide an entree to a subsequent meeting.

One sales athlete I know never approaches a client prospect without a referral from someone that prospect knows and likes. Certainly a phone call that begins "I was talking to your tennis partner, John Bancroft, and something he said led me to believe you could benefit from our services" is more of a buffer than "I'm representing the Acme Disposal Company, and would like the opportunity to show you our new product line."

Premium Buffers

Few people can muster references for every client they access, but other types of buffers can be even more effective.

You can buffer yourself from rejection through cold-calling if you send or have dropped off inexpensive but thoughtful and unusual gifts that send a message: "I care about you, I'm not here to bother you, I'm going to give you something back for your time." If, for example, a client prospect brusquely rejects your first telephone call or visit, follow it up with a second touch that he or she will remember.

Some examples I've used with great success: A lottery ticket, taped to my calling card, along with the message: "Take a chance!" Or a car windshield guard that will keep the interior of a prospect's car cool and that pulls out with a message about how to best use my services. In the wintertime, my current favorite is an inexpensive one-cup coffeemaker, with my calling card and motto affixed to the handle. The coffeemakers help me to shorten accessing time with targeted accounts.

If it's the holiday season and your client prospects are swamped, send along a candy cane in a red cellophane wrapper with a heart sticker. The message: "Let's take a few minutes and I'll show you an idea to help parlay the profits of this holiday season into a more profitable Valentine's Day [or February]."

I may not always use my buffers, but the fact that they're there for me makes me feel more confident while I'm pursuing new contacts. Any inhibition toward approaching new contacts will always impede your progress toward achieving personal and professional goals, but if you equip yourself with verbal and premium buffers, you'll never need to humiliate or make a pest of yourself with relentless phone calls to the same client prospect. Buffers are dual-purpose tools that protect you from fear *and* create access to new prospects.

Of course, sensitivity must be used when choosing buffers. Misused, they can offend rather than attract clients. I wouldn't send a lottery ticket to anyone I might suspect would be offended by gambling, or invite someone to a meal unless we'd already met and established a potential business relationship. **Caution:** Always be certain your premium buffers reflect good taste, professionalism and the image of your company.

Most of us have read about and recognize in our own lives the importance of first impressions. In accessing new contacts, it is crucial that your first impression create trust, establish rapport and lower resistance to your request for an appointment.

If you are calling in person your manner should be relaxed but respectful. If your attitude is presumptuous ("I like you, therefore you must like me, and I am free to relax with you as I would with a trusted friend") you may engender mistrust and resistance.

Once your well-chosen buffers are in place, you can forge ahead with accessing hard-to-get prospects, who frequently have their own buffers in place to thwart your approach.

Mike O'Brian, publisher of *Sacramento* magazine, called to retain my services in order to help one of his account executives get over the fear of making in-person cold-calls. Both Mike and I had called upon mentors to help us with this beginner's problem; now Mike wanted to give this very talented young account executive a mentor.

The woman explained to me she had been accustomed to prearranging her appointments and felt that cold-calling (arriving on the premises of an account without an appointment) was demeaning. She admitted to feeling foolish saying this, but nevertheless it was how she felt.

I outlined to her the Sales Athlete® "touchdown" strategy and how to use verbal and premium buffers. We set up an appointment for the next day to review what had happened when she cold-called five prospects and to go over the answers to a list of questions I needed her to answer before we designed a "touchdown" strategy appropriate for her targeted prospects.

The questions:

— Do you believe in your product, and why?
— When is the next Chamber of Commerce or association gathering of your targeted accounts?
— Who are the owners of your targeted accounts? List their names.
— What are the most demeaning and frightening moments you could experience with these prospects?
— What transpired during your five cold-calls? Bring me the calling cards of the people you met from each call.

At our follow-up meeting we reviewed the five cold-calls. She had not made contact with a single owner. There would be a Chamber of Commerce meeting on Tuesday at 8:30 A.M., following a 7:00 A.M. meeting of its retail committee.

The young woman's worst fear was that her ideas would go unappreciated when cold-calling on prospects—they would send her signals that she was an annoyance, a pest.

Employing the Sales Athlete® strategy, we wrote each targeted account a letter introducing her as their new account executive, and made special note that she was looking forward to meeting them at the upcoming meetings. We mailed the letters and three days later, armed with a pocketful of scented wooden acorns from my reservoir of premium buffers, we took to the streets cold-calling together.

I reminded my young client to realize that her first touch had been her letter and that her second would be to visually assess each retail store, along with the type of merchandise it carried, and to identify the location of the owner during the day. When the owners were not on the premises or were "hiding," she was to leave the store's manager with an acorn and her calling card with a hand-written note that said "From acorns mighty oaks will grow—I have an idea that will take only a moment of your time."

At the end of two hours we had covered over

ten stores, met four owners and sold one contract for $12,000.

"Target your associations and go for the very best," advises jingle writer Danny Obst, who has sold his creative work to Tyco Toys, McDonald's and Yamaha Motorcycles. "Go for the hardest accounts to get." If you never tackle these prospects, you will never find out how easy it actually is to reach these key decision-makers.

Think of the friends you always call who are unavailable to you on the first try. My own biggest client is a woman with heavy account responsibilities: I'm lucky if I reach her twice out of ten tries. Similarly, because I do so much corporate lecturing, if she tries to reach me ten times, her odds of getting through to me are just as low. Yet this is a relationship that is crucial to us both: We *want* to reach each other. Therefore we keep on trying.

I think of this relationship when I'm prospecting a new account and trying to connect my timing with their timing, and need to fight back disappointment when the prospect is unavailable.

The ideal is to leave a message that piques their curiosity and holds their attention long enough to get a call back.

"I've got a Christmas present for you in July,"

for example. My prospects as well as my loyal clients have told me I leave the most interesting and effective messages on their voice networks and with their secretaries. These verbal buffers serve my prospects' and clients' best interests, shorten my selling cycle and help me avoid disappointment and the sinking feeling of personal rejection.

When I really have to reach someone immediately, I send a fax of an eight-by-ten telephone message sheet (these are available from the Think Big Company in New York City). The oversized message, with appropriate boxes checked, reads: "Please call. I will not steal a single moment of your time."

If you look at accessing as a challenging sport rather than as a potential traumatic experience, you'll be better prepared to keep coming back to prospects even when your first couple of tries meet with rebuffs.

Jingle writer Obst begins accessing difficult prospects by creating allies within their firms—particularly the secretaries whose job it is to fend off salespeople. He is so friendly and thoughtful, the secretaries and assistants are happy for him when he finally makes it through to the big boss.

"I treat them as if they are as important to me as the guy who has to say 'yes,' because in effect, they are," Obst says of executives' first line of defense.

"They tell me exactly what I need to do, because I treat them with respect," he adds.

When he does get beyond the secretary or assistant and actually sets up an appointment, Obst says, "I always include the secretary in the win. When I finally get through, I say, 'You have to come to the listening session—I couldn't have done this if it weren't for you.' "

When facing a particularly difficult prospect (in Chapter 5, I refer to this type as the "rude and crude" prospect), it helps to shield yourself with the attitude employed by publisher Karen Fund: "I think of them as a boot, and of me as a sponge. I get booted by them, but my sponge envelopes the boot. I can take as many blows as they want to put out because I just embrace them."

Many times, Fund says, this image helps her turn difficult prospects into "not only very large clients, but friends."

Some of the most valuable prospects are simply not accessible through normal channels: approaching a receptionist, establishing rapport with a secretary and then moving on to her boss. When you're hoping to close a $1.5 million contract, accessing just may have to be done through the right country club membership, or a 7:00 A.M. tee-off Thursday with your client prospect.

CHAPTER 5

Building Contacts

Once you've built up confidence in yourself and your game plan, what stands between you and the finish line? Chances are, even when you've gained solid confidence in your own abilities and have great enthusiasm for what you're selling, there are still situations in which your first instinct is to run, cry or get angry.

Think about what triggers that emotional response. What if seven prospects in a row tell you they consider both you and your idea a waste of their valuable time? Does that make you want to go home and crawl under a blanket, eat a double fudge sundae or go on a shopping spree?

Maybe you *are* able to move smoothly forward

through outright rejection—but what really gets you down is the prospect who listens politely for a half hour, then can't make up his mind and wants a month to think about it. You can picture him drifting, drifting away, along with the precious time you feel you've just wasted.

True sales athletes cut right through these frustrating situations and turn seemingly hopeless sales scenarios into profitable business relationships. How? By quickly identifying and adapting to the six different prospect types.

The six types of prospects and their responses (verbal or implied) are:

1) Skeptical ("I don't believe a thing you're saying.")
2) Indifferent ("You are a total waste of time.")
3) Indefinite ("Maybe I'd be interested but I don't have time right now.")
4) Rude and Crude ("Didn't you see the 'no soliciting' sign? I don't care what you're selling, I don't want any!")
5) Interested ("I'm so glad you called—today's a perfect day!")
6) The Objector ("I like the idea, but it seems so expensive . . . it doesn't fit . . . is it guaranteed?")

Try to think of a seventh type, and you're likely to come up with somebody who has combined aspects of all the above responses. You may have an indifferent prospect who repositions into a skeptical prospect who moves on to become an interested prospect—or a skeptical prospect who becomes an objector . . . and so on.

You can buffer yourself from feeling rejected by viewing accessing your prospects as a safari. The sport is in identifying and labeling prospect types, then letting the labels be your guide to tried-and-true approaches for bagging each type of "game."

Any time you approach someone with a product, service or idea, your prospect will respond in one of six ways. Put more simply, there are only six types of game you'll ever meet in business. With practice approaching each of these six types, you remove whatever fear you may have about approaching any and all kinds of prospects.

The different attitudes of your prospects require you to treat each one differently as you go about your job of getting and holding their attention. Identifying a prospect type is really not so difficult if you consider that you yourself bring to each situation a different aspect of your personality or perhaps a combination of attributes: At the office, the efficient professional "you" is very much in evidence, but with family or friends other traits appear.

Assessing prospect types and adapting a presentation to suit each type is an exercise that completely engages the sales athlete's intellect. It requires great skill and patience—and it's fun!

The role you play in this exercise is not to memorize a scripted presentation and then give that presentation by rote, but rather to consistently identify the kind of individual you are currently communicating with and creating a flexible, adaptable game plan appropriate to each prospect type, never relying on hackneyed "pitches."

The first step in dealing with prospective clients is to gather all the information you need about them. The second step is to gain an overview position and assess their type. From there, design a presentation specifically to meet your clients' needs. Instead of rejection setting you back, you'll begin to see the challenge in adapting your approach and establish the rapport and lowered resistance to the presentation of your product, service or idea.

Now let's take a more detailed look at how each of the six client prospect types operates.

1) *Skeptical prospects,* for example, believe they have good reasons to distrust you and whatever it is

you represent. A skeptic does not believe a word of what you're saying—a person who strikes at your very fiber by calling you a liar or insinuating you are not telling the truth. It's very easy to become defensive and respond emotionally.

Recognize, though, that by the time you meet him, the skeptical prospect may already have been ripped off by three or four salespeople that day. His car turned out to be a lemon. The office duplicator doesn't work and nobody answers at the repair number. He feels a little sheepish about having believed the last guy, who turned out to be a phony with a cheap product and a worthless guarantee.

Because you understand exactly why he may not believe your sincerity, you don't take his attitude personally. You meet the challenge and provide the proof this prospect needs to feel comfortable with your idea, product or service.

What you need when dealing with a skeptic are three absolute truths—indisputable, credible facts—that go right to the account, served up as proof to overcome the prospect's belief that you are trying to take his money and give him less than value in return. So from your handsome attaché case, or from the superbly organized trunk of your car, you whisk out your "skeptic emergency kit."

It includes as much proof as you can gather from three sources that your product, service or idea has been tested, is of current value, has been enjoyed and pronounced by others to be desirable and of the finest quality. Not six or seven facts—wouldn't that look defensive?—but three. As time on the job goes by, you will collect many facts for your kit. Three will usually move this prospect to listen.

You might include articles from industry or general business magazines showing your product to be on the leading edge of its field, or testimonials from front-runners in the skeptic's business who have found success with your company. You want statistics, testimonials and articles to back up a clear, positive and friendly presentation of your product, service or idea.

As you see, instead of putting your energies into an emotional response to the skeptic, you focus on putting them into turning the skeptic into a trusting objector. Then, you can meet his objections.

Skeptics are the prospects most likely to feel you are not like them. By looking, acting or talking like a "typical" salesperson, you can actually create a skeptic. By appearing as much like your prospect's best customer, however, and creating a skeptic emergency kit to fit your prospect, you can usually get a skeptic's ear and win his trust.

I carry not only a thick, fact-filled skeptic emergency kit, but also different presentation folders to visually lower resistance. Is the prospect a dreamy, creative soul or a banker type? I can pull out the granite-imprinted folder, or one with black, pink and red leopard spots—or a plain old manila folder if I'm not certain.

I always separate the presentation of my skeptic emergency kit from corporate folders provided to hold my presentation because I believe the kit lowers resistance as I present the facts it contains.

The moment you hear over the telephone a skeptical prospect, pull out the appropriate kit and ask, "Are you still located at . . . ?" Explain that you are going to send in the mail the three facts appropriate to your presentation, and describe each fact. If you speak confidently—remember that your intonation and attitude are amplified over the telephone—you will find a more trusting prospect listening to you. Then you can suggest you stop by to offer your presentation in person; the skeptic will by now be more receptive to taking time to see you.

2) The *indifferent prospect* is the most commonly encountered prospect type. It's easy to see how your emotions can kick in with this prospect. Here you are, a reputable sales athlete with no intention of stealing

a single moment of his time and he doesn't even want to come to the phone or into the reception area to meet you. The indifferent prospect is absolutely confident, absolutely positive you have nothing to contribute in any way, and therefore sees no reason for spending any time with you.

He will tell you this in a variety of ways. He may say, "Listen, we don't use those, we don't want those. I'm satisfied with my existing resource." The prospect will send you a signal that you can contribute zero to the well-being of his organization. When this happens day in and day out, some salespeople develop a reluctance to make calls because they don't know how to lower the number of indifferent responses. If you are one of them, let me show you how to turn your "flight" response into positive actions.

I would like you to place your right hand across your chest in a stance similar to the one you would use for the Pledge of Allegiance. Then, with a backhand movement to the right, see yourself separating yourself from all other "sales" people. Not just from all other salespeople in your industry, but from *all* salespeople who have ever called on this prospect. You're going to place all those salespeople over in a corner, and walk toward the prospect not as a sales *person,* but as a sales *professional,* ready to identify and solve problems. Now is the time to draw from your collection of verbal and premium buffers.

First, verbally separate yourself by offering a low-stress benefit that proves your request is a productive use of the prospect's time.

Your opening statement might be, "I'll bet you have a lot of salespeople calling on you."

"I sure do—bet we've had one hundred today," the indifferent prospect might snap.

The sales athlete says, "But there's a difference. I don't have to fill out a call report. I'm not calling on you to help fill out my call report. You're telling me that if you let all of these people steal your time, you wouldn't have time to do your job. If given a couple of minutes, I promise I will not steal a single minute of your time, in fact I guarantee it."

The prospect's assistant might be acting as an abrasive go-between, separating you and your prospect: "I know he's not interested," she snaps before you've been able to completely identify yourself.

Jump right in there with assurances: "Eight hours a day I work with people like your manager who are struggling with the same industry problems—I want to make sure your manager has this competitive information."

Verbal buffers are never first rehearsed on your prospects. They are collected and role-played with your peers, managers and counselors.

3) The *indefinite prospect* is more likely to induce a sigh of exasperation than a spasm of fear. Here is a type the sales athlete does best with if he prepares a good offense.

If I could draw a picture of the indefinite prospect, it would be of a giant snail. These are the same people who can't even make up their mind about where to go for dinner.

"I hear you," you respond to his balky indecision. "You want to lay this idea out so it's easy for you to understand. Now, do you have your calendar in front of you? Pen handy? Okay, see you Tuesday at 10:00."

Don't give him two choices—lead him. You can't do that with a skeptic or an indifferent or interested prospect, because you'll risk their becoming defensive and escalating into a rude and crude type. With the indefinite prospect, as my grandmother trained me, "You never push a noodle—you pull a noodle." Pushing a noodle would be to make your presentation aggressive, from the standpoint of your own interests, seeming to care nothing for the prospect's needs. Pulling it would be to gently lead the prospect your way.

Your role as a non-option leader is restricted to the indefinite prospect. The no-choice strategy forces him to take action.

4) The *rude and crude prospect,* on the other hand, evokes an image of a mad, barking dog. This thought may make you cringe, but whenever I meet a barker like this one, I want that customer!

Rude and crude prospects are loyal. Because they won't stop to listen to new information, they frequently remain uninformed about available improvements. They cling to existing services.

But once you win them over, however, rude and cruders are yours forever. These prospects will not hesitate to tell you what they need to keep them loyal.

Remember when facing a nasty, obnoxious character like this that he didn't save that behavior or create it just for you. It is something he uses regularly as a business method because it keeps people away. Rude and cruders believe their behavior works because it does succeed in creating a distance between themselves and any perceived outside threats.

Once you recognize that rude behavior is not directed at you personally, however insulting it may be, you can tailor your game plan using techniques familiar in the martial arts. A basic principle in martial arts is to avoid the blow. The art is to use your weight as a lever in overpowering the attacker.

While I don't suggest using this particular strategy on someone with a knife or gun, I know that most sales athletes find it works, and it is what they use to establish rapport with a rude and crude prospect. The reason these prospects are rude and crude is to get you to go away; when that doesn't work, they frequently will listen to your presentation.

A prime example of this type came my way recently. In soliciting a new prospect I reached his secretary, who recognized my name from having taken the Sales Athlete® training program. She identified me to her boss with more than my name, because by the time this prospect got on the phone he was primed and growling.

"You got a tickler?" he asked, referring to the old-fashioned calendar file system.

"Yes, I have a tickler," I responded.

"Well, put me down for July 23," he snarled. "And when you call, I'll be sure not to be here!"

I replied, warmly, "Ouch! Mr. ——! Please! You may not want to do business with me now or at any time, but I guarantee you that you don't want me to leave this conversation angry, when my intention is to help you generate more sales."

With that, I heard him loosely cover the mouthpiece of his telephone and shout to his secretary, "She got me! The Sales Athlete® got me!"

At other times, when a rude and crude prospect comes snarling and barking my way, I might look aghast, shake my head and quietly say, "Let me load a gun and shoot whoever hurt you! This is not a normal response to a call from me. You must have had a terrible experience. Tell me about it."

Once again, I've separated myself from all other salespeople. Once that barking dog is calmed, take good care of him and he'll become a happy, loyal client.

I let these prospects tell me how they've been ripped off, how all salespeople are conniving, how they're not about to let me try and con them into something they can well do without. I encourage them to vent their frustrations. When they are through they usually feel a little silly—not only were *you* listening, they were listening to themselves too, so now they are willing to listen to what you have to say.

I let these prospects know that I, too, am angry at "those people" in the past who have let him down. It is people like that who are preventing them from listening to the advantages of my services.

5) Compared to the wafflers and the barkers, the *interested prospect* must seem like a gift from heaven. Isn't this a salesperson's dream come true? "I'm so glad you called—today's a perfect day!" When you hear those words, be grateful—but beware. Some-

times, prospects are so interested, they don't give you a chance to sell. That can leave you with a sale, but what a sales athlete wants is a satisfied, loyal client.

Never take an interested prospect for granted. Qualify an interested prospect by asking, "Tell me, why did you decide to call us today? What do you like most about our service?" The information given to you will identify the prospect's needs, give you information about their need that can be useful testimonials to skeptical prospects.

Aren't you continually turned off by retail sales clerks who ask, "May I help you?" If, however, the same clerk were to ask, "What made you decide to visit our store today?" you probably would respond more positively and with something specific: "Your window display of leather jackets."

A sales athlete always appeals to the pride of interested prospects. He or she does this with "statements of gain" such as: "You made a good decision stopping in to see us today—let me show you our selection of leather jackets."

A sales athlete also brings out into the open any objections the prospect might have, and is prepared to meet those objections. Why? Because the biggest misery and the hardest bills to collect stem from people who start out so interested they buy a product or service without being sold on exactly what to expect. Their initial interest is sparked by a fantasy that the product or service will deliver something it may not in fact deliver. Had they been sold, they would know exactly what to expect. Instead, they wind up furious to learn that what they bought doesn't give them the satisfaction they expected it would.

This lesson was brought home to me *very* painfully. We had a person come into our service from the television production industry. In this field you may work six weeks, then you may look for work for a year. We just happened to have a client who wanted to produce a magazine-formatted television program. They wanted someone "connected with the networks" who could take the idea of the show, translate it into a saleable project and get it on television. The job paid a $60,000 base salary, and the client was about to turn in his Jaguar, so the car would go to the sales athlete placed in this position. *And* the job was bicoastal—zip! zip! across the country at will. This lucky candidate got the job with no sweat.

It so happened that he was also president of an entertainment-industry organization at the time, and stood up at one of its meetings shortly after he got the job and told this entire group of two hundred industry aspirants about his good fortune. Naturally, he enthusiastically sold our service as the referral resource.

Imagine fifty people all pushing for a job when only one had existed and was already filled. These callers had no idea what our service did, no idea of how we conducted business. All they knew was that we could deliver a $60,000-a-year bicoastal job with a Jaguar, selling television programming.

We began requiring that everyone coming into our service sign in and tell us whom they were referred by. Whenever we spotted someone who was referred by the man who got the TV job, we went out of our way to explain exactly what services we provided. Until we did that, these referrals were leaving skid marks outside of our offices. They had bought our program as interested prospects—prospects interested in getting a $60,000-a-year job with a Jaguar.

To this day, these people pop up in my life, and the problem is that they were sold something we in fact never packaged as part of our program.

So when a prospect acts interested in your product or service, you must always do your best to *qualify* their interest.

6) The very best prospect is, in fact, the *objec-*

tor—a potential client who is clear, positive and friendly and tells you why an idea doesn't work for him and under which circumstances it would.

Once you have gathered all the information you need to meet the objectors, you will be stimulated—not emotionally drained—by the fulfilling activity of turning your prospects into satisfied clients. You don't have to trick anybody into buying, you simply have to identify and meet their needs.

The sales athlete's task with the other five prospect types is to bring them to the point of being objectors—encourage them to trust you and tell you what their true feelings are, what they want and expect. The approach with skeptics should be to earn their trust so they can tell you their objections. You want rude people to focus their real objections. You want indifferent people to listen and then tell you their objections. Why? As long as you are dealing with an objector, you can meet his objections and turn them into a sale. The objector himself will always tell you what he needs.

Sales athletes know it is unwise to sell something to a person who genuinely does not want or need their product, service or idea. They are quick to determine, through rapport-building information gathering, how much of a prospect's resistance is based on hidden emotional factors rather than objections that can be satisfied.

To a sales athlete, the world is not a threatening field of barking dogs and well-guarded opponents. What's out there are companies and individuals who really *need* their products, services and ideas.

CHAPTER 6

Winning at the Sport of Negotiation

Styles of negotiating move through time like trendy phrases in our language. If I said "Hot diggity!" you'd think "1950s." If I said "Far out!" you'd think " '70s." The expressions come and go, but we add them to our language and continue to use them to evoke the tone or style of a different era.

Likewise, new tactics and styles in negotiation develop as corporations merge or as politicians forge policy with competing interest groups. Henry Kissinger added "shuttle diplomacy" to the lexicon of negotiation. Ollie North's habit of asking his interrogators to "please explain" (causing them to reveal bits of their strategy) added "controlled deniability" to the repertoire of negotiation tactics.

An abrasive, aggressive power management style was popular in the late '70s; in the '80s, manipulation was added—salespeople would back prospects into a corner, in effect trapping them into closing a sale. Today, as more and more workers apply for stress-related disability payments, there seems to be a lot more honey on the tips of corporate tongues. When companies consult with me about hiring sales managers, the first thing they want to know is: "Do they stress their employees or do they coach them?" Nobody wants an intimidating manager, and prospects are too sophisticated to fall prey to aggressive, power-grabbing salespeople.

So what approach should we take as we segue into the 1990s? What's the best system, the style, the attitude—what are the maxims—that will keep us in synch with these times? We think the approach is embodied in the Sales Athlete® training principles: Establish rapport, lower resistance, build loyalty.

Loyalty: Taking customers from year to year rather than starting each year as a clean slate.

To develop loyal contacts, we need to learn how to negotiate, which, at its best, is a process that bonds people to one another. The sales athlete's goal in negotiating is to produce a result in which each player leaves the field with a satisfied feeling of goodwill toward all parties involved in the negotiation. At the end, all the players have succeeded and have bonded together in the process.

Most of us, however, have not been trained or encouraged to take advantage of negotiating opportunities. This culture, unlike most others in the world, courages negotiation. We are taught that "haggling" or bargaining for products and services is somehow unseemly—if an item or a service doesn't cost or doesn't deliver what we'd like it to on the face of it, we go elsewhere. We are neither encouraged nor trained to negotiate, and negotiation is a skill that requires both. It might even be called a sport.

There are three major phases in the sport of negotiation:

1) The Imperfect Situation—Recognizing there is a problem to be negotiated and deciding to begin the negotiating process.
2) Discovery—Assessing the strengths and weaknesses of the negotiating parties.
3) Satisfaction—Completion of the negotiation.

Because many people have not been taught to negotiate well and are not comfortable with the process, they avoid negotiating altogether rather than moving from the first step to the second and then to the third. Or they become impatient to reach a settlement, and give up before both sides reach satisfaction.

I have watched some people who when offered a job that pays $30,000 plus a commission take that job without negotiating. These people earn exactly what was first presented to them.

Other people negotiate. In the process of testing the flexibility of the salary and benefit package, the prospective employer—instead of becoming angry—feels he *must* have that skillful negotiator working for him.

"If he's dribbling *me* around the office, I can just imagine those negotiating skills when turned loose in a territory!" the employer thinks.

I've also been in rooms with people yelling at each other—and have found out later they were actually having a great time negotiating. Negotiating can be a lively, creative process.

Successful negotiators are not born, they're trained. People who learn the sport of negotiating sell more, earn more and in general get more of what they want in life.

Opportunities to negotiate are everywhere, as

I learned in my first encounter with a negotiating pro I'll call Lillian:

I moved into an apartment in New York, bringing along my prized collection of carnival poster art and antiques. A new neighbor, Lillian, flew into the front door, looked at my things and pronounced, "What you need is some new furniture."

I was taken aback, but so as not to alienate anyone in my new neighborhood, I responded politely, "What do you suggest?"

Within minutes we were in her car, headed for this "fabulous discount furniture store." All during the forty-minute drive she told me about the deals and opportunities that would present themselves to me when I finally got to this furniture store that she'd been going to for years. We arrived, and from the moment I stepped inside it was obvious they didn't have a single thing that would fit my decor. We walked in, though, and she saw a piece of furniture that went from ground to ceiling and from one wall to the next of this large showroom—one of those "stereo lifestyle units."

Lillian began the negotiating dance the moment she looked at the price tag: It was a $7,000 item marked down to $3,500.

She said to me with a wink, "Go and find the

owner." And, not realizing the game had begun, I raced off and came as close as I could to satisfying her, which was to find the owner's son.

Lillian then entered phase two of the dance, saying to the man sympathetically: "I bet you don't sell a lot of these." He shrugged. Pointing to the vast area taken up by the lifestyle unit, she said, "It seems to me you could put a couch right there and another one there instead, and sell at least two every week."

"Well, yes, the unit's on sale," he conceded.

Moving into phase three, Lillian said, "I'll give you $1,100 cash for it."

With an initial reluctant sigh, the owner's son looked at Lillian and said, "Today's your lucky day. $1,100, but don't tell your friends."

Then we approached the counter. Lillian added, "And you'll deliver it." And he said, "That's $95 for delivery."

"Forget it, then," said Lillian, snapping her purse shut with a sweet but firm smile. At which point he folded, and agreed to eat the delivery charge.

"I think this piece of furniture *belongs* to someone as tenacious as you, ma'am," he concluded.

To this day, Lillian has a negotiating trophy in her home that overpowers all other furniture in not just her living room, but the entire apartment.

We moved from the furniture store to a major department store, where Lillian spotted a magnificent red dress on a mannequin. She asked a saleswoman to take the dress off the mannequin and took it into the dressing room to try on, ordering me in the meantime to "go get the buyer." When I hesitated, she shouted over the dressing room wall: "Buyer! buyer!" and the buyer soon arrived.

"This is an interesting color of red," Lillian told her.

The buyer, attempting a compliment, said, "Not many people have your color of skin that makes that orange-red look so beautiful." Lillian pointed out that the dress was made for a short-waisted woman, and that because she is short-waisted, the dress would be perfect for her.

A perfect color, a perfect fit—shouldn't that be a sale?

Lillian said, "I bet you don't have many people who come in with short waists and my color of skin and hair."

And the negotiation began. Lillian said to the buyer, "I'll give you $375." The buyer said, "The dress is $850, but you're right, it does suit you perfectly. I'll mark it down to $450."

Lillian, holding her ground, handed the buyer

her calling card and warmly said, "I'm afraid $375 is my limit. When you have to beat your department's previous year's figures, and you need this sale to meet your sales projections, call me." At which point the buyer whipped out her pen and discounted the dress on the spot.

Mind you, the buyer too was having a good time. Lillian was having fun. Throughout it all, Lillian joked, "This is your lucky day!" And the buyer responded with a chuckle, "I need this luck?"

What I learned that day is that *everything* is negotiable—except stop signs and red lights.

I was thinking, "Can I ever come back to this store? I'll be too embarrassed." Lillian, however, is now considered a preferred customer there. She and the buyer bonded through this experience, because both are professional negotiators. The process—the bonding—had nothing to do with the dress itself.

I've told that story at many department stores and the presidents have smiled and said, "We like Lillian." Because Lillian had brought to her negotiations a genuine understanding of the problems faced by sellers, they appreciated her bargaining strength.

Despite my initial embarrassment, Lillian turned me into an avid fan of negotiating. I developed a voracious appetite for negotiating aids. I began buying books, identifying tactics in negotiation, labeling them, observing and making special notes of tactics I saw used successfully in business and on the evening news. Negotiating tactics are the "art" I collect to this day, and negotiating has become the sport I most enjoy.

Today, as part of my service I'm continually required to negotiate compensation plans and reconcile problems for clients. Although I don't have a shingle out that says "professional negotiator," my clients have naturally gravitated to me because of the way I've negotiated with them for consultant services and fees.

Many people miss negotiating opportunities that could enhance their personal and professional lives. Their notion of negotiating conjures up negative images: fights, confrontations, power plays that might make them feel stupid. It irks them to go out and ask for things they feel they shouldn't have to ask for. The goal of this chapter is to remove those emotional reactions to negotiating so that you can begin to use negotiating skills with the agility of an athlete. With practice, you'll come to see negotiating in the most positive light, as a loyalty-generating sport.

But let's not confuse this sport—negotiations that bond, win respect and create loyalty—with "dirty tricks." If you are interested in bonding through negotiation, eliminate any thought of using tactics that will make people resent you. Nasty moves may produce a short-term win, but they ensure that you'll never engage in the sport with that player again.

The sport of negotiation is a lot closer to dancing than fighting—there are no winners or losers in dancing. After a good dance, as after a good negotiation, both partners walk off the dance floor satisfied.

Training for the sport of negotiation begins with an active recognition and use of tactics. You'll be on top of any negotiation procedure if you have as part of your equipment a bag loaded with negotiating tactics.

Once you recognize and identify the moves made by you and your negotiating partner, you'll be able to view the sport intellectually rather than emotionally. When you remove your emotional response, what's left is your intellectual best. Negotiating is fun because it begins bonding people to you. When done well, it establishes loyalty and cements long-term relationships.

How do *you* feel about negotiating? Many of us approach negotiation from an uncomfortable emotional position, because all negotiations begin with an imperfect or unsatisfactory situation that requires you to take action if it is to be resolved.

To help yourself identify and begin removing blocks that keep you from enjoying satisfying conclusions to your negotiations, ask yourself the following questions in this negotiation "physical":

1) *Do you feel in control or effective in some negotiating situations, but at other times feel absolutely limp?*

Negotiation is a trained sport that brings into play your intuitive skills—and your intuition is the sum total of what you know. If you are trained in how to buy a home or a car, you will feel comfortable doing so. If not, you should pay someone—just once—to take you through that type of negotiation step by step, detail by detail. Make notes about some of the things you don't know how to negotiate: salary? car? house? divorce? rent?

2) *Do you sometimes fail to recognize negotiating opportunities?*

We negotiate whenever we have an imperfect situation, and we negotiate until we find satisfaction. Our bodies have a way of telling us—sometimes through clenched fists or upset stomachs or a desire to run away—whenever we're in an imperfect situation.

Many times as you are closing the products and services you represent, you will be tapped at and tested with objections identifying what it is that will satisfy that prospect: "It's too expensive," or, "I need it Friday," or "This one is white. I need half of them in blue and two cases of yellow." So you want to finesse satisfaction on the part of the prospect, as well as to yourself and to the service, product or company you represent. You want to ensure a "win-win" situation. If you negotiate well, all parties come out better than when they went in.

3) *Do you feel you lack the skills to negotiate well? Would you prefer others to negotiate for you?*

Recognize now that you *can* teach yourself these skills, and that if you don't, the *most* expensive services you will ever pay for are those requiring negotiation skills.

4) *Do you get embarrassed at the idea of negotiating? Are you afraid to ask for what you want?*

Perhaps as you were growing up you were disciplined in such a way that discouraged you from negotiating. A friend told me that as a child, he asked his father for a bicycle for his birthday, and his father responded, "You ruined the surprise, so I'm not going to get you a bicycle after all."

Years later, my friend remained afraid to tell anyone what he wanted for fear he wouldn't get it. Many of us inherit problems through such negative discipline, when our parents did not know how to respond to our testing of their power. You're mature enough now, however, to say, "I *can* change that," and no longer avoid negotiating opportunities for fear of being reprimanded or disappointed.

I'd like you to become eager to negotiate—unrelenting in the pursuit of getting everyone a good deal. Look at it this way: If you can't negotiate a problem, you've got a problem. We're in executive communications, so the people we trash with problems are powerful. Sales athletes recognize that a failure to negotiate can leave behind a trail of conflict in their careers, and who can succeed with that?

How to Tackle (and Employ) the Most Common Business Negotiation Tactics

In order to negotiate successfully and to buffer yourself from experiencing the negotiation emotionally, you must learn to recognize and develop negotiating tactics. Once you have used a tactic or experienced it being used on you, you can *label* it as such. That tactic then becomes just one in a series of possible plays—part of the negotiating game—rather than an attempt to wound or overpower you personally. The following twelve tactics are major negotiating skills.

Tactic 1: Delay

When you have the power, use it; when you don't, delay.

Say you start a job in which you are promised a salary review and the opportunity to make another $1,000 a month after six months on the job. You go into your manager's office and say, "Well, it's my six-month anniversary. Could we please discuss my salary review?"

He says, "I just don't have time now, but I'll get back to you shortly."

A week goes by, and he says, "Give me ten days—I'm going out of town." Now you're over the moon with frustration, because you've been delayed.

Presidents of companies often can negotiate a contract with an entire foreign country, but cannot negotiate a simple compensation plan with their secretaries. This supervisor may be delaying because he doesn't know how to negotiate with you. He needs to be taught *how* to give you a raise.

When people delay, they frequently need more information to get them "unstuck"—with all the necessary information before them, it will be more difficult to justify a delay.

My suggestion in the case of the salary raise would be for you to go back into the manager's office and say, "I have a feeling you've been delaying this because you need more information from me. And you'd feel more comfortable if I gave you more information about why you should give me a raise."

You might prepare a grid illustrating every month you've been working down the far left side, with the amount of money earned per month. Another sheet would show the number of hours worked per day, the number of accounts and dollar volume of the accounts. On the next page would be another grid, showing in blue the income you've brought into the company, and in the green the income you've earned.

Give your supervisor a copy of this material and say, "I know you have to go through channels, so you could just attach a memorandum to this if you like." You have empowered him with information.

Tactic 2: Silence and Bracketing

Coupled with a tactic called bracketing, silence is very, very powerful. Information gathering is best achieved through silence. When we bracket the attention of the information giver or person we're negotiating with, we direct their concentration to a specific area of the negotiation, then listen aggressively—carefully, silently and without jumping to respond—to everything they have to say on that subject.

If I simply say, "Let's discuss for a moment a succulent, juicy hamburger," and then I'm silent, you would fill that silence with your gut-level reaction to the specific issue of juicy hamburgers. Your response might be, "Oh, the *best* hamburger I ever had was at Joe's, and now you've got me craving another one." Or, "I don't eat meat, and the very mention of that turns my stomach." Whether your response is positive or negative is not the point: I have *bracketed* your attention to the subject, then used silence for a period to retrieve information regarding how you feel about the subject.

Silence and aggressive listening give the sales athlete as much information as possible in a negotiating situation.

Bracketing can also help the sales athlete target and recognize what information he or she is missing in order to present a product, service or idea.

I myself use bracketing while presenting the Sales Athlete® corporate training services to a new account. First, I introduce myself as the founder of an organization that trains sales executives in some twenty-two different skills related to executive sales communications and to enhancing sales productivity, lowering turnover and increasing profit. Then I'm silent, listening to where the prospect is in terms of his sales training needs. I give him an overview, then bracket his attention to three subject areas, using silence and aggressive listening to gauge his response and need for my services.

Tactic 3: Limited Authority

We've all heard this one: "I'll take this upstairs and see what we can do." "I've got to talk to my partner." "My agent makes those decisions." "I've got to send that to my lawyer."

When you've reached a point of closure and are stopped by the limited authority tactic, most likely your prospect *has* the authority, but has discovered some objection to your product, service or idea that leads him to this point of impasse. Your move is to discover what that objection is by "repackaging" the information for the person of supposedly higher authority.

Example: "You want to review this with your attorney. How does your attorney best like the review information for his approval?"

Your prospect responds: "Well, I send it over, and he reviews it, and sends it back, and we review it together over the phone."

You say: "Well, I'd like to give you the information to present your attorney. What do you suggest I emphasize?" And reposition your presentation so that it removes any mistrust and any misunderstandings that hold potential legal problems. Because you've intuited that what he's said to you is that he doesn't trust your presentation is legally in order.

If you suspect it's the client's accountant who needs to review your proposal, ask "In what format does your accountant prefer to evaluate projects?" Once the person tells you the objections he feels his accountant will have to your presentation, you can reorganize your material as though you were presenting it to the accountant.

You are actually engaging in role-playing. Your prospect takes on the persona of the accountant—or spouse or partner or attorney—and you reorganize your material as though you were presenting it to this invisible third person.

When the invisible objector is "my partner," you ask, "What aspect of the business does your partner oversee?"

"Administration." You would then refocus your presentation as though you were presenting it to an administrator. You may actually even engage in a little outright role-playing: "Let's say you were your partner, and I were presenting this to you. . . ."

Tactic 4: The Bottom Line

This is the point below which you will not go. If the bottom line is that you can't discount a product, all of your energy must be put toward selling it for full value. You've likely heard the adage in sales and marketing: "If you have two aspirin in your pocket and don't know how to sell them, you might as well take them for all the good they'll do you." The bottom line is that you don't waste time redesigning aspirin, you direct your energy toward selling aspirin to people who need aspirin.

Whatever your product, service or idea, at the bottom line there is a price and there are benefits. The strategy is to identify people or organizations that need it, can afford to pay for it and can abide by the policies and procedures of the organization that employs you.

When you're negotiating, and you hit your bottom line, you cannot charge any less or redesign your offering. When you accept the bottom line, your creative problem-solving strength is directed toward those prospects who need and want what you are selling.

The bottom line is your scorecard—the description of your product, it's pricing, corporate policy regarding credit terms, volume, availability, delivery time, guarantee and quality assurance. The configurations of these components determine the bottom line for sales athletes. The key is that you go into negotiations fully understanding what your bottom line is, and prepared to ascertain the bottom line of your prospect.

Imagine a client says his fiscal year ends December 31. The company wants your product but wants you to come back January 1, and here it is October 1. Their unspoken bottom line is that they won't have any money until January 1. Between October 1 and January 1 your competition could come in and usurp this client's enthusiasm for your product. Therefore you may want to talk to your manager and see if you can arrange a purchase order with credit terms—buy now, pay ninety days later.

Or a client company says, "I can get your product cheaper elsewhere, and I must buy on the basis of price only." In fact, you know your product withstands heat, cold and pressure, or has a benefit above all the other products in the field that justifies its higher price. The sales athlete would take any extra steps to ensure that all client prospects in that company are aware they are not able to buy *your* (better) product cheaper. You'd pull out that benefit. Your bottom line is that you won't discount, so you use creative problem-solving skills to justify the pricing of your product and close the sale.

Tactic 5: "No"

The great value of getting a "No" from your prospect is that you can ask "Why?" and everything he tells you in response comprises precisely the circumstances under which he will buy. A "No" thus doesn't signal the end—it is the point at which the prospect trusts you enough to tell you he is not going to buy. "No" can be parlayed to a point where true feelings are disclosed, bottom lines are revealed, and where it becomes clear to you what objections you must meet in order to sell your product, service or idea.

Tactic 6: Nibbling

Children are experts at this. Nibbling is the ability to withdraw and then return, but keep the pressure on:

"May I go to the movie?"

"First clean your room, and I'll think about it."

(Five minutes later) "May I go to the movie, please?"

"Well, did you clean your room?"

"No."

"Clean your room first."

(Ten minutes later) "I *almost* finished cleaning it. Now may I go to the movie?"

In sales, you can use nibbling as a positive negotiating tool to continually keep the subject in front of the prospect until the problem is resolved. The "touchdown" strategy requires nibbling. You can nibble as you relate to your territory like a cop on the beat, continually going back to check on client prospects, seeing them and also being seen.

Tactic 7: Expectation and Control

This is where you say, "This part is not negotiable, but that part is." All of your prospect's energy becomes redirected to the area that is negotiable. You let the prospect know what the product does and does not do, so that the prospect is not blind in his belief about your product. This is positive, clear, friendly and honest.

Tactic 8: Auction

"I can get it cheaper (better, faster) somewhere else. . . ." This is the single most powerful tool in the hands of a buyer. If you don't know your competition, or don't know what mood they're in today, you're up against the auctioning tactic.

When confronted with this, ask what the cheaper rate is. Give your prospect more details of your presentation. Explain that the price is not negotiable, but that something else is (a better service contract, the color choices or the delivery time).

You might say, "This is how we do business—we have trucks that work, that send our product out on time, people that stand on the docks to ensure quality control. Our competitors don't. If you're at all concerned that things might shut down or a problem be created for you should our product not arrive, we're going to ask that you consider paying a little more to make sure it does arrive on time."

Tactic 9: Concessions

Concessions, however slight, should be given very carefully, treated like gold, wrapped in silver and presented like a gift to a monarch. They can be the key to bonding a relationship in negotiating.

Always keeping in mind the reverse pyramid method of account service (we described this in Chapter 4), your goal must be to convince your prospects you are working *for* them. Concessions can help you do that—if you present them carefully.

Frequently, a mistake is made in the guise of "inducement closes." A prospect has decided not to buy, and has said something like, "It just doesn't fit." The salesperson then throws in an inducement: "If you buy it by Friday, I'll give you 10 percent off." Meanwhile, the prospect still doesn't think the product or service fits his corporation or his equipment. Salespeople may have a whole list of valuable inducements and just throw them on the prospect's desk in hopes that something will induce a sale.

Use concessions to *build* interest. That way, you can also withdraw them. You say: "If you buy five dozen, you get a display rack." The prospect says: "I'll take three dozen and a display rack." Your response is: "No, I'm sorry, I have to withdraw the rack offer because we have found that if you commit to five dozen you will build repeat business. If you buy only three dozen you won't have the depth of merchandise necessary to generate repeat sales, or to develop a reputation of being a vendor of this item."

You have offered a concession, then taken it away, thereby creating an incentive for buying on your terms and getting the concession back.

Tactic 10: Rationale

If in fact what anyone is looking for in negotiation is satisfaction, recognize that satisfaction doesn't necessarily have to be what the person is asking for.

I divide my time between lecturing and corporations. A very big problem with my work is that when I'm giving a presentation to corporations I can't take phone calls, and when I'm with a corporate client I also can't take phone calls. This means I am not always reachable. Phone calls usually come from people with a problem. At my office, therefore, there must be someone who can handle the callers so that, although they have asked for something (to speak to me) and have not received it, they leave feeling taken care of because they have been given a ractionale that satisfies.

If you are to make a mistake in negotiation, it should be that you give too much rationale that satisfies rather than not enough. I once thought someone was absolutely ripping me off. The client said, "Let me break it down for you," and when he gave his rationale, the reality was that I was not being ripped off. I left satisfied even though I did not get what I originally thought I should have gotten.

Frequently people are remiss with creditors because they are embarrassed that they cannot pay their bills. If, however, they pick up the phone and say, "Listen, there's a strike, I cannot pay in full, but let me work something out" they can negotiate to everyone's satisfaction through rationale.

Tactic 11: Message-Sending

During negotiations, messages will come your way verbally, visually and in writing. Understanding this tactic is crucial to reading your adversary.

If all of a sudden someone stands up and looks jittery, don't talk through it. Recognize that something has just transpired. Read the nervous laughter, the jiggling foot. If all of a sudden someone starts crying—and that has happened in negotiations—the response to the message would be not to concentrate on price or services, but to move the person from an emotional position back to an intellectual position.

People send written messages, usually of a less dramatic nature but needing to be read with the same sensitivity as visual or verbal cues. A client you've been doing business with for years stops returning your calls—that's a message. Or pays his bills more slowly than usual—that's a message.

Tactic 12: Deadlines

The sales athlete tests them all and understands their roots. Frequently deadlines are artificial. They can remove profitability from an account, and when you test them you learn they are in fact there because of the belief that you won't service on time.

"I need it Friday."

"Why?"

"I'm going on vacation for three weeks." That's a deadline.

"I need it Friday."

"Why?"

"We go into production Tuesday." That's a test. To which the response might be, "Well, to get it to you Friday, we will have to FedEx it, which is an extra cost. You'll either have to pay or it will remove the profit from us. Whereas if we send it our usual way, we guarantee it will get there by 9:00 A.M. Monday, which is twenty-four hours before your production start."

Those are just the beginnings of a grab bag of tactics you'll see and use in negotiations. Once you begin recognizing and labeling such common moves, you'll see how much fun it is to identify and name your own. Labeling tactics makes them easier to tackle and helps you to buffer yourself from interpreting them emotionally.

With a knowledge of tactics in place, you are prepared to enter Play I of negotiation, which begins the moment you find yourself blocked into an imperfect situation. Your first play in the game may begin with something as straightforward as, "I like the idea of your service, but it's October 1 and we're spent for the year, so I can't buy until January 1."

In active negotiation both parties acknowledge it's time to negotiate. Once the problem is brought out in the open, each comes into the negotiation equipped with tactics learned from their own experience.

Upon entering negotiation you bring all the skills of a sales athlete together—training, timing, patience, an overview perspective.

Once you are in the game, all of your mental energy must be focused on making each play successfully. Like a quarterback during a football game, you must concentrate not on the final outcome, but on keeping the ball. In the words of sales athlete Marty Weiner, "My goal is not to win, it is to never miss."

Your success in negotiating also depends on your ability to gather as much information as possible about your negotiating partner's needs and goals. Information gathering is crucial during Play II.

In lawsuits, this stage consists of the expensive and time-consuming process of taking depositions. It's called discovery, a time for getting to the bottom line. In business, you go back and forth showing each other the ways in which each of you will reach satisfaction. It is the "who, what, why, where and when" stage. The most successful player here is most often the one who listens best.

In Play II, you'll use your strategic, analytical and tactical skills. The goal of this stage is to evaluate your own strengths and weaknesses and those of your negotiating partner and to ascertain the *real* (as opposed to the expressed) desires of your prospect. ("I want a discount" may mean the prospect really wants to be satisfied that nobody else is getting a discount.)

You've identified the imperfect situation: Your prospect says he wants your product, but it is October 1 and he cannot pay until January 1, so he wants you to come back then. (Delay)

You say: "You'd want us to install in January?" "Yes," he responds. "Things could change, but I would like to evaluate it for January 1."

You say: "It's within our capabilities to deliver November 1 and bill you in January—would you be interested in that?"

"I have to check with my manager." (Limited Authority)

Your retort would be: "You would have a sixty-day trial period and if it met your expectations, you would pay for it on January 1."

"All right, I'll get back to you," says the prospect.

Next you're back in your office and the phone rings, and on the other end of the phone is the prospect, who says, "I spoke to the management, and they are concerned that at the end of sixty days we won't like it but since we've used it, we'll get stuck."

Your prospect is still interested, your strengths and weaknesses and concerns have been aired, and now you are ready to enter into Play III—settlement.

Impatience is the greatest impediment to satisfactory settlements. In Donald Trump's book, *The Art of the Deal,* he describes how it once took three years of patience to get from the first play to the second in a multimillion-dollar real estate negotiation.

Stage one gets you in the game, stage two into establishing positions. We know we're well into the third stage of negotiation when one person establishes dominance over the other.

Your prospect says, "Our management is concerned that if we install this in November, we won't like it and we'll have to pay." He is trying to establish dominance by persuading you to extend your guarantees.

You could end this negotiation by any of the following ways:

• Pacifying—When you accommodate, or settle for something. "I lose, you win." Impatience to reach settlement is the enemy that will lead you to this unsatisfactory conclusion.

You could pacify the prospect by throwing in a concession: "Our standard guarantee is if, for any reason whatsoever you're dissatisfied, you won't have to pay. And if it really is of such concern to you, we'll deliver in October. You don't have to pay until January." Clearly, in this situation, you lose and still have an imperfect situation.

Instead, you could "gift-wrap" the concession, making clear it is a valuable trade-off, not a throwaway. "We would agree to put in writing that if the equipment is installed in November and it doesn't live up to its promised performance, we will replace the equipment free of charge."

• Compromise—This is the so-called happy medium settlement, in which you walk away feeling you lost, but at least everyone else did too. So many negotiations end like this, yet if both parties had the patience to see a problem through to satisfaction, they could reach a winning settlement. Now the prospect says, "I think I could get it through my management if you gave us a ninety-day guarantee instead of a sixty-day guarantee." He wants a guarantee not through January, when they pay for it, but through February 1.

"Fine," you could say, in order to compromise and expedite the sale, but you still would not have a losing proposition. Instead of pushing for the sale immediately, you could say: "What we're interested in doing is extending our usual credit terms (a concession) so that you have full enjoyment of that equipment through the months of November and December.

"We want to give you the benefit of using the product through January, where normally, we would require a one-third payment at the time of the order, a third upon delivery of the order and a third in January." Let the prospect know your firm has already given a major concession.

The prospect then says "Great!" to your offer, because he was just pushing to test your limits, and knows that he is now getting a good deal.

Had the sales representative said "Yes" to the push, he would have walked away without a win-win settlement, with the prospect in an unnecessary position of dominance. And, if the salesperson had made that concession, the prospect would have continued to push for more concessions. This is a negotiation tactic frequently used with salespeople. How do you stop it? Make concessions rarely, carefully, only when you have to. Never just "throw them in, and keep a scorecard."

• Cooperation—Sales athletes have the persistence and patience to cooperate toward a settlement that is satisfactory to all parties. You keep at it, and when your prospect seems unable or untrained in the sport of negotiation, you ask, "Are you really satisfied? Let's see if we can't work this out so you're satisfied, rather than tired."

Have you ever negotiated a deal where you gave a client everything he wanted and he *still* didn't buy? Most likely, that occurred because the client didn't leave with a sense of satisfaction.

The sales athlete engages in principled negotiation, as it's referred to in the excellent book *Getting to Yes* by the Harvard Negotiation Project.

To reach a cooperative settlement in which everyone walks off the field feeling like a winner, you don't have to intimidate or manipulate anyone into a box. The tone of the sales athlete in negotiation is the tone of an equal and sensitive partner or a patient teacher. It is warm, and filled with regard and respect. It is the tone of a seasoned executive communicator.

PART IV

Career Security

BUILDING CLIENT LOYALTY

CHAPTER 7

Avoiding Sales Career Injuries

The way we react to failure is as crucial to our success as achieving success itself. Do we admit to our mistakes and get the help we need to move on? Or do we allow failure—or the fear of it—to stop us in our tracks?

Just as runners or tennis players risk injury if their training lapses, sales careers can suffer debilitating setbacks if training is ignored.

I've counseled hundreds of people whose sales career injuries have led them to feelings of confusion or depression. Frequently their mistakes have led them to wonder whether or not they should try another profession—rather than commit to continued self-training that will avoid sales career injuries in the future.

There are the obvious, colossal injuries: drinking so much at a party that you throw up on the hostess's couch or have to be carried home; sleeping with an important client, who the next day stops returning business calls; allowing yourself to vent your personal frustrations on a client in the form of verbal abuse. Counseling or a vacation may be required to remedy such injuries.

When commitment to training is undertaken but then lapses, executive sales careers show symptoms that are less dramatic, but insidious: After four years on the same job you lose the passion you once had to pursue new accounts and take care of loyal clients; you experience a setback in your personal life and allow your appearance to advertise your sorrows ("So what if I have a run in my stocking or a stain on my shirt? Nobody cares. . . ."); you forget to congratulate your best client on his son's high school graduation, or neglect important clients when sending out invitations to a big, talked-about bash.

Such symptoms viewed singly may appear to be minor injuries—slipups in details that are chalked up to a "bad day." Sales athletes are aware, however, that such symptoms are signs of losing their competitive advantage. Painful as they are, sales injuries can serve as valuable tip-offs that it is time to get your training program back on track.

Your attitude is critical. If you lose the courage or the desire to embrace each moment in your career as an opportunity, it is crucial that you recognize the lapse and do what it takes to pump yourself up again.

What chance for success is there if you carry around the kind of attitude that shouts, "I don't care. I'm bummed out. This bores me (makes me uneasy, irritable)"? As many times as you may have heard it, I'm going to tell you again: You can't win if you think or act like a loser.

You are doing the job you chose to do, so relax and have a good time—enjoy yourself! If you do, clients will too. Even if they don't buy from you immediately, they'll at least like having you around, and they'll invite you back.

What we represent to our client companies is a persona that has attracted clients and their loyalty over the years, and developed a reputation for reliability. Sales athletes keep training to keep in shape. They are always on top of their clients' industries, flexible and able to foresee and fulfill their clients' changing needs.

Probably the most important sales career injury I see is inflexibility. People who learned something twenty years ago, who think it's still working that way today and insist on training people within their compay the same way. These are people with a blind spot to the need for continued training. When a company is failing, sales athletes know why—it is usually failure to be open to new information.

I see this frequently in my open-enrollment classes, when five out of seven people on a company's sales staff show up over a period of time for training. I tell them it would make much more sense to custom-train the whole organization. Then I find that the president of the company, who fashions himself as a sales trainer, is completely closed to the idea that any new training is needed. He continuously manages with out-of-date, proven ineffective sales methods. Yet more than half of the people on his staff come to my classes on their own because they see the need to self-train.

I've also had inflexible client prospects sit in front of me and declare proudly, "Our biggest asset is our reputation in the industry." They are completely blind to the fact that their reputation is one of high turnover, cruelty and draconian collection practices.

Sales athletes, however, come to me eager for any bit of fresh information because their attitudes are open and inquisitive. They walk in like breaths of fresh air—presidents, regional VPs or other consistent top producers in their field. They are quick to identify ineffective clichés that have slipped into their presentations.

To avoid injuries to your sales career, choose your mentors carefully—role models who serve as examples in areas where you may be inexperienced or insecure. Human beings are imitative creatures by nature, so we should surround ourselves with people who succeed at what we want to learn to do.

Most sales injuries come from an inflexible attitude and failure to pay attention to the following areas: pacing and balance, training, attitude and style, and relationships. We hope a look at some memorable sales injuries will help you avoid suffering your own.

Pacing and Balance

We would like to think we have much more control and much more energy than we actually do. The fact is, even if we're in peak condition, our days are only twenty-four hours long and our energy is limited. Therefore, to do what we love most about our career requires pacing to avoid depleting our resources. Overextending for long periods—"burning"—leads even the most talented of people to become mentally and emotionally exhausted, less able to make decisions and less effective in maintaining relationships.

What sales athletes do automatically at the end of every day is evaluate what has been taken out of them, then replenish it. They recognize that their job is physically and emotionally demanding and that to be fresh every day you must put back what you take out.

If you knew you were going to take on an assignment that would mean putting eight normal days of work into a five-day work week, you would have to pace yourself. That would mean not eating foods that require extra energy to digest, not giving up your half hour of exercise in the morning, not wasting three hours of the afternoon because you drank too much at lunch. The buzzword is balance: balanced meals, balanced activities, balanced life.

If you are to operate from the philosophy that if you burn for a day, you must rest for a day, what are you going to allow to burn you? It may be that meeting a deadline on a year-long project or consummating a deal with your company's most important client is enough of a priority in your life to throw you off balance, yet you accept this willingly. But stretching your limited resources to that extent should be done only by choice, not by default, and not routinely.

Having a system to organize and prioritize your time, and paying attention to planning your day on the basis of balanced priorities, will keep you flexible and help you avoid burnout. It will also allow you to set aside time to recuperate psychologically and physically from those rare occasions when meeting a goal has meant depleting most of your energy. Leave behind the idea of "control" and in its place put "prioritize." Prioritizing allows you to be flexible—control implies rigidity and inflexibility.

A client called me once saying, "I need to replace so-and-so." "Where are things going wrong?" I asked. The client explained, "We're closing the month and this guy asks me to go on a sales call with him, puts me in a car where we're out of commission for two hours, to a client that couldn't buy more than one case. The way he wastes time is driving me up the wall!" Disorganization and failure to prioritize his time were the sales injuries that cost that unfortunate salesperson his job.

When checking references, I often hear this: The person looks great, has a terrific personality, but can't get on top of projects and has a poorly organized territory. And without that organization, the person has no energy left for creativity—a vital ingredient in a successful sales athlete's career.

Failure to balance your personal and professional life can lead to divorce or unhealthy relationships with your children, creating worries that in turn cause you to lose passion for your work. If you become a workaholic or try to be superhuman, you'll appear manic or harried, detracting from your charisma and causing you career injury. A sales athlete understands that you can—and should—ask for help: Delegating makes the people around you more competent and frequently adds more enjoyment to their works.

Time management systems were designed so people could avoid spending most of their energy trying to be very busy, since it's known that extremely busy people are frequently ineffective workers. "Don't confuse activity with achievement," suggests successful jingle writer Danny Obst.

As discussed in Chapter 3, sales athletes prioritize their activities with the help of a time management system. The system keeps them in check. When too many "priority A" activities pile up on a single day's schedule, or when it seems that "priority C" activities never get attention, the sales athlete changes the priority of some activities or reschedules things in an effort to avoid burning out or burning his clients.

Training Injuries

Unless you continue to self-train you'll run the risk of winding up like Willy Loman—out of style, out of the running. Just as a 1970s wardrobe will cause clients to doubt your ability to stay current, and therefore strain your credibility in general, failure to keep current with your industry, your competition, your product and negotiating skills will be noticed and cause you eventual injury.

When you stop exercising, your muscles become stiff; when you stop gathering information necessary to your career, you will lose the underpinnings of career security.

People who stop get stale. Everything is always changing, and the stakes keep getting higher and higher. Remaining uninformed will surely lead to unemployment and disenfranchisement from your accounts.

In the film industry, says producer Doris Keating, "you see a lot of monsters made" by failures to keep in training. "People don't keep their looks, don't keep abreast of information that they're required to. There is no finish line. There may be a series of plateaus, of resting places, but basically, this is a marathon that doesn't finish until you finally check out."

Stockbroker Latchezar ("Lucky") Christov, a sales athlete who managed to succeed with his own new firm the year his industry was reeling from the October 19 market crash, says he won't consider hiring anyone who is a sort of "mechanical salesperson"—a person who relies solely on his company's daily research reports for information, "who may not really understand what it all means or what part in the industry it plays."

Christov not only reads everything he can get his hands on relating to a company of interest, he gets close to the company's president ("I sleep with management," he jokes) and each morning makes up to a dozen telephone calls to clients around the country who keep up with the market and sector trends.

"I don't call people just to chat," he stresses. "They're busy too."

Training should always include regularly attending seminars and association meetings and reading industry materials. I am amazed at the number of sales managers who believe that to read magazines or collect information is something that should be done outside of office hours. Sales athletes recognize the critical need for fresh information in order to remain flexible and on top in their careers. When a magazine comes in the morning, they read it the moment it arrives to help identify problems in the industry and creatively solve them. Information gathering should be continuous. It should go on during every sales call and between calls.

Not keeping up with information from newspapers and magazines, not participating in industry association meetings, not continually training and retraining yourself will make you "out of it," stale, a cliché. Clients will identify you as someone who uses "fillers," who is poorly read, clueless.

You can say "I just picked up *Marketing Week* . . ." and use that remark as a means of connecting with a prospect. If you allow publications to stack up in your basket and let the information get stale, what do you suppose will be the impression you make if in March you say "I was reading in last November's *Ad Week* that . . ."?

Information gathering must include knowledge about your competition. Read their advertisements in the trade publications. Review their booths at trade shows. Stand toe-to-toe with their sales representatives at association meetings. Identify their strengths and weaknesses—in procedures, pricing, corporate policies, products, even the personal habits of the sales representatives and their managers.

Attitude and Style

Of the thousands and thousands of requests for executive communicators I have received, I have *never* received one that said, "Send us all the bitter, tense and obnoxious ones. People who have an accusatory, hostile manner."

We are in the business of negotiating. We're executive communicators, and conflict is contrary to who we are. I cannot further the career of a difficult, inflexible person. Bad attitudes create conflicts in offices that redirect everyone's energies into placating the difficult person rather than solving problems that bring profit.

Sales athletes don't walk around with phony grins, glad-handing everywhere they go; they genuinely feel the passion for their work that brings continued success. Most importantly, though, they have the social sensitivity to know that even when they're a little low on energy or enthusiasm, it pays to act as if they're not. If you've tried this, you'll know the miracle that occurs when behaving positively actually lifts your spirits and creates positive feelings.

No amount of skill in your profession can compensate for a bad attitude. My service tackles many,

many problems created not by a salesperson's poor production but by his or her poor attitude and style. Employers will say, "He brought in five orders this month—that's not the problem. It just isn't worth what he's doing to the rest of the department and what he's taking out of me with his pain-in-the-neck personality."

Clients will frequently identify a problem by referring to an employee's "chemistry." When I hear that, I know the problem is with attitude or personality. A rude or testy attitude with a secretary can permanently block access to a key decision-maker. A failure to move through your fears and build a self-confident attitude can cause you to hesitate in approaching new accounts and targeting key decision-makers.

The importance of style—including appearance, manners and the personality you project when doing business—cannot be underestimated. Even laboratory scientists, research engineers or others in low-visibility jobs will enjoy more success in their fields if they are able to communicate with style. In executive sales, the ability to do so is crucial to vocational security.

Just as I began writing this book, the president of a major temporary employment service telephoned with a request for a branch manager because he had ruled out considering an existing employee for a big promotion. Why? When he took her to lunch to discuss his plans for her future, she picked up a steak knife and sliced her bread lengthwise, instead of tearing a small piece off with her hand.

It seems like a trivial thing, this fine point of table manners. It was important enough, however, for this manager to look closer and determine she lacked the sophistication necessary for the job he had in mind. Their lunch conversation took on another direction. No style, no promotion. Ouch!

Another woman, nationally recognized in the media industry, suffered a career injury in my very presence. (Had I not been there, I would never have believed this one.)

I was in Atlanta, Georgia, sharing a lectern at an association gathering with this media leader. At lunch, she ordered scallops—the tiny bay variety that come forty or so to a plate. The moment lunch was served she began to devour every one of her scallops at breakneck speed. This assault on her lunch, however, did not interfere with her animated conversation—until a piece of food shot out of her mouth and stuck to the eyeglasses of the association president.

I didn't realize it at the time, but I was competing with this woman to give the association's national address, an opportunity to appear before hundreds of influential people and earn a sizable fee in the process. I definitely was not as prominent as she; all she would have had to do is eat properly, and the opportunity would have been hers. Instead, her shooting scallops led to one of the more important junctures of my career.

Inattention to appearance can also cause critical sales career injuries. There is an actress seeking my services, for example, who has fantastic contacts and who will someday go far, I'm convinced. But she wears false eyelashes and outlines her lips in black pencil over pale pink lipstick. She tells me she gets interviews but that nothing seems to work out. I reply, "I'm positive we can solve that," and I hope she'll pay attention when I gently tell her why.

Women with plastic fingernails, men with long sideburns, people who dress too casually or twenty years too young: All seek career guidance when what they need is to develop an appearance that establishes rapport and lowers resistance. Their questionable dress code stands between them and the message they are trying to deliver.

Sales athletes don't send out symbols that one shouldn't trust them because of what they're wearing. Certain symbols instantly create a sleazy impression:

long or unkempt fingernails, giant pinky rings, black shirts, white ties, too much makeup, too-tight clothes, a wardrobe that is out of date or so trendy it works against your credibility.

Frequently, people are unaware they are sabotaging themselves with their appearance. All of us can benefit from regular consultations with someone who cares enough to honestly critique our appearance and wardrobe.

Consider a yearly "makeover" or "appearance physical" with the help of a friend who has impeccable fashion taste, or with a personal buyer or fashion consultant from a quality department store. These must be people you trust can be honest with you, who care enough to say "Don't ever wear that again" or "That hairstyle has got to go."

Women who refuse to shave the long black hair on their legs, men who haven't changed their hairstyle since the '60s or who refuse to cover the tattoos they got when they were drunk at nineteen should not be surprised when their company finds an unrelated reason to fire them. And you can bet that competitors both within and without their companies won't care enough to tell them the real problems they've caused themselves.

A good appearance and style extends to your

sales equipment. People have been fired on the spot after negotiating a sale to the point of signing a contract, then discovering they forgot to bring one. A smudged or wrinkled brochure is as unforgivable as rumpled clothing. A car that isn't maintained can cost thousands of dollars in sales. Outdated technological equipment will give your competition an instant advantage.

People who affect a serious "business voice" with their clients, or a tone that is inappropriately seductive, hilarious or insincere certainly do themselves injury. Would you trust someone who sounded like a phony or who didn't have the sense to speak to you straightforwardly, without leering, giggling or snickering?

Never forget your style and persona, even when you're "not working." You never know who may see you walking around the neighborhood on Saturday morning, or call you at home and hear the message on your answering machine. (One employer told me he was ready to hire someone until he called him at home and heard W. C. Fields on tape singing, "I'm a party boy, if you're a party girl.")

I once attended an industry event being held in a club where everyone had to walk down a steep staircase to get to the valet. The woman leaving the event in front of me was well known, well respected—and obviously drunk. She weaved down the stairs, going back and forth between the handrails, finally stumbling and landing at the bottom flat on her stomach, with her dress over her head.

At the top of the stairs were ten industry shakers staring at this woman. I rushed to help her up and into a cab.

This incident occurred eleven years ago, and people are still talking about it. It's been repeated to me in so many versions that I find myself simply responding, "I don't believe a word of it—it's simply impossible."

The woman who suffered the injury, meanwhile, left town because a repuation as a drunk left her unemployable. She went from being the first female senior executive of the number-one company in her industry to another company in an ancillary industry in another city.

Relationship Injuries

Relationships are crucial to everything the sales athlete does. What makes you a sales athlete is your ability to establish rapport with new prospects and build trust and loyalty. Relationship building is so critical to fulfillment in both your career and personal life that inattention to your relationships can cause the greatest injuries to your career. Never let down your guard. Sales athletes maintain a mystique that sets them apart from everyone else.

In executive sales, you'll frequently find yourself in dozens of formal and informal social situations with clients and prospects, and walking the line between friendly conversation and conversation that is too personal can be quite difficult.

"To reveal too much about yourself or to let [clients] reveal too much about their life is a great mistake," warns Karen Fund. "You'll regret it and they'll regret it, and you're likely to lose business in the process."

For example, a woman I trained had gotten to the final interviewing stage at a major news magazine—one of those job opportunities that comes once in a lifetime. The person interviewing her was at the time embroiled in a political brouhaha at his office. During the interview, because the prospective employee was so adept at establishing rapport, the employer used her as a sounding board and laid out every bruise in that company. Because the woman didn't know how to shut that conversation down, leading the interviewer gently away from conversation he'd later regret, she wound up in a position where she couldn't comfortably be allowed into that organization.

"It's very hard, very seductive," adds Fund. "People are talking to you, you want to be as close as you can with people. It has to stay friendly, but not personal."

Obviously, "personal" includes any sexual or romantic advances. Dating clients is just too dangerous—for your business and your reputation—to be considered.

Remember the key strategy of targeting your relationships that we outlined in Chapter 2? Forgetting it can be a source of continuing sales injuries.

Many salespeople walk into a company and find someone they like, and because the prospect is so kind and the atmosphere so warm, they spend time there and return, even though the prospect may be unable to bring the volume of business needed to reach the salesperson's goals.

"A lot of salespeople think because they're going through the rudiments of it all, they're doing their job," says Danny Obst, who sold advertising specialties before concentrating on selling his music. "If they're not targeting their efforts to the right people, they're just going through an exercise in futility.

"You have to be competitive. You will get what you go after. If you go after bad clients, you get bad clients. Target your associations and go for the best—why not? Go for the hardest to get. The only thing that makes them the hardest to get is the perception that they're hard to get. But they're just human beings, like everyone else."

Once you have targeted your client relationships, it is imperative to take care of them and not take these hard-earned contacts for granted.

I am currently consulting in a major "injury recovery" case involving rapprochement between a large company and its former best client, a major corporation.

The injury? Last year, the wife of the corporation's president sent invitations to a $150-a-head fundraiser to benefit a charity for a disease. Everyone who received invitations from this woman was expected to help sell tables for the benefit. Incredibly, though the corporation is a $15-million account of my client, my client sold not a single ticket. Not only that, but his secretary, when called by the corporate wife spearheading the benefit, was told, "Sorry, but we don't have that as an approved charity."

Over the next seven months, millions of dollars' worth of business has been drifting away from this "insensitive" company. My client, faced with laying off fifty employees and losing prominence in his industry, wasn't aware of what went wrong. By asking around, he and his people finally figured out that the cause of this severe injury was their ignoring the favorite charity of their best client. The injured company is now frantically scheduling a whole series of events to bring this account back on board, giving it the opportunity to say a dozen times, "We didn't realize what had happened."

Invitations to charity events don't come from out of the blue. When they come to me, I always look down the list of sponsors and send at least a donation if a client is involved and I can't attend.

Need we point out injuries caused by lying? When you lie, you die. The best story I know to illustrate this comes from Arthur Pardahl, a media director for years at the Foote, Cone and Belding agency in New York. I walked into his office one day and saw an enormous medieval shield of armor on his wall.

"God, Arthur, where in the world did you get that?" I asked, as everyone who entered must have also. And Arthur told me the story.

"This kid came in here," he said, "and had the gall to lie to me about his publication's circulation, as if I'd been in the business two days. He insisted that his circulation figures were accurate. I banished him. I said, 'You told me a lie—you can never come back into this office.' "

By way of apology, the young man sent Arthur the shield. The price of that lie? Every person who walked into Arthur Pardahl's office heard about it. Arthur would not tolerate misinformation, and he used the story—without revealing the young man's name—to impress everyone with that point. Anyone in his office would then think twice about exaggerating.

Breaching a confidence is as injurious as lying. I have heard of one salesperson who was fired after going into an office, putting his material down, then purposefully picking it up and walking out, along with the top-secret material that was underneath it.

Most sales injuries don't put you on the bench for life, but recovery can be hard. Recovery begins by making amends, like the young man did by sending the shield to the person he'd offended.

I just heard a story about a new sales recruit. On his first day, he didn't show up. It was suicide. I immediately put his file in the "never again" folder, and set about trying to recover the trust of the company that had hired him.

Later, he called to say he was in a 12-Step program and wanted to make amends to all the people he had harmed. The company was empathetic on the telephone, although not completely forgiving.

I've on occasion picked up the phone and said, "I'm sorry," only to have someone lash back at me.

"That's why I'm calling," I'll say, "so you can tell me." By apologizing and giving the person an opportunity to vent his or her anger and frustration, I hope to begin patching up any problem I may have caused unintentionally.

Once you've honestly admitted your mistake, recovery is possible if you immediately bend over and do back-flips in the service of your client. Quit hiding in embarrassment and get to work doing something so well it will astound your client and the competition.

Remember the Tylenol disaster? How on earth could a company recover from such an injury—the poisoning of its product? It recovered by an all-out effort to win back consumer confidence. The company didn't attempt to calm people's hysteria by belittling their concern. Instead it tested, then wrapped and sealed and double-sealed its product so tightly it could barely be opened, let alone tampered with. Tylenol not only recovered, it won consumer confidence in the process.

Never underestimate your own powers of resilience or your ability to turn a bad situation into a positive one. It may take agility, flexibility and creativity to make a stunning comeback after an injury, but it can be done.

I know a sales athlete who was calling on a client to sell him advertising space in a trade publication. The salesperson had neglected to read his own publication that morning, which included a scathing editorial reference about his client. When he walked in, the company president sputtered and spat: "Did you see *this*? All morning I've been getting calls from my best customers over this editorial, and you want me to buy advertising space?"

The sales athlete, agile and flexible, responded calmly. "I regret the article," he said. "Regrettable and forgettable, thank God. However, the fact that all of your best customers have called clearly shows our publication reaches the people you want to reach. I think that instead of buying a six-month contract, we should talk about a contract for twelve." The company president reconsidered and signed a contract.

The media, by thriving on people's errors, has produced the expectation that no one can make a mistake and survive. We live in terror of making mistakes, believing recovery is impossible. Sales athletes avoid major career injuries, but they also realize that some of the greatest learning experiences come from picking ourselves up, dusting ourselves off and starting again.

Mistakes, awkward situations, even out-and-out disasters can put us back on track and in training. Sometimes, as in the Tylenol case, they work to our ultimate advantage. People have been fired and, while recovering, discovered exciting new careers. Sometimes it is our ability to recover from painful mistakes that shows us—and others—how flexible and strong we really can be.

Sales athletes recover quickly from their mistakes by welcoming the lessons they teach. They neither expect themselves to be perfect nor allow their imperfections to stand in the way of their progress.

CHAPTER 8

Keeping Clients in Good Shape

The dynamics of being a successful sales athlete require gathering timely information on a playing field far beyond the usual office setting or business lunch. It may extend to a golf course or boating club, to parties, association meetings, weekend retreats or events that join new clients to the family of satisfied, well-established clients.

It is hard to believe, but some industries discourage business entertaining. They dress their sales representatives in uniforms that mask any personal style, and send them out to develop new business for their companies. How can these representatives compete with a socially savvy sales athlete?

A client, shell-shocked by his business losses, called me, lamenting, "I'm sick of fickle clients!" A close look at his involvement with his customers showed he had done nothing to promote or earn the loyalty of his customers. While he could name the companies he depended on for income, he could not name ten of his largest accounts by the name of the decision-maker.

The purpose of wining and dining clients is to build trust, solve problems, pin down details and create a receptive mood in which to do business. Sales athletes seize every opportunity to build loyalty with their clients. No matter how well established the relationship, they never stop trying.

Clients prefer to do business with people who understand their problems and who can be trusted. Sales athletes choose careers in which they feel they'll enjoy the people they do business with. As a result, many times clients become friends, and business relationships are cemented through mutually shared social occasions.

Sales athletes do business in a way that enables them to keep showing up at the country club or can look clients in the eye at church on Sunday. Their only hidden agenda is selling ideas to people who need them and enjoy their loyalty. The aim is to create a client base that will enrich their professional and personal lives and ensure their vocational security as long as they choose to work.

If you engage in a sport with a client, attend the same special dinner party or belong to the same club, you have made an inherent pledge to perform. When your client is a fellow club member or tennis partner, the pressure is on in your business dealings to provide not simply a product or service, but to provide a good deal. Clients like to do business with salespeople under that social pressure.

To perform under that kind of pressure, you'll need to include in your training a variety of social skills—from knowing how to throw a great party at home to knowing how to choose the best table at the restaurant best suited for power entertaining.

Let's begin with the most basic things—manners and meals. Although "power lunching" seemed destined for the fad heap a few years ago, the practice of cutting deals over meals still thrives. Nowhere is etiquette—or the lack of it—so visible as at the dining table. While sharing meals with clients bonds you together, it is far easier to create social distance during the course of a meal than it is across the client's desk. (Remember the incident of the "flying" scallops in Chapter 7?)

Manners are an awkward subject to discuss, because reminding adults of certain points of etiquette—

where, for example, to put the napkin when you leave the table to take a call—strikes at their very upbringing. Judging from the frequency of corporate requests for my "power entertaining" seminars, however, I have found that many people—executives included—want and benefit from brush-up training in the area of social etiquette.

We are very rarely told about our transgressions, but people can think about them all the time. Talk with your mouth full or make a lesser faux pas at a meal, and your client won't say anything but will go away thinking, "Oink, oink, oink!" He'll never remark about your bad manners, but he'll certainly remember them.

There is an art to getting your point across at breakfast while keeping the egg off your face. It begins with the choice of restaurant and table, and concludes with the manner in which you pay the bill and exit a parking lot or cab.

Here are some basics your mother probaby *did* tell you about (understand that only a friend would remind you of them again):

• Don't pick your teeth. Not with a toothpick or a fingernail. *Not even just once.*

• If your guest has a piece of food dangling on his chin, remove a phantom one from *your* chin with your napkin. If that doesn't work, softly say "Only a friend would tell you . . ." and repeat the gesture.

• Once your napkin is placed on your lap, it should not reappear on the tabletop until you are ready to leave the restaurant. If you must excuse yourself during the meal, place your napkin on your chair.

• Wipe your mouth often during the meal, and always before you sip a beverage. If you're in the middle of a conversation, in fact, you might want to limit yourself to your beverage, to avoid the awkward pauses necessitated by chewing or, worse, bits of food flying across the table.

• Small bites will allow you to swallow easily and to speak as you eat. Tear bite-sized pieces from your bread, one at a time. Never cut your bread with a knife or bite off pieces from a whole dinner roll.

If you have any trepidation about your table manners with a client, buy a book of basic etiquette, study it and practice with a friend. Not all of us, by any means, were brought up knowing the difference between a fork for shellfish and a fork for salad, or taught the proper way to eat pasta.

Once you have confidence in your ability to comfortably negotiate your way through a meal at the most elegant restaurant, it is time to consider the finer points of power entertaining, which include the debate over drinking and mastering the "bite count."

If you are a drinker, the rule of thumb to remember is this: Never drink over one drink more than that consumed by the person you are with. If you have a glass of wine and a client has a glass of wine, he might think less of you if you had another, and what would he think if you had three? However, if a client wants to have three, you really don't need to have more than one—sip yours slowly so you keep your head and you're keeping him company.

If you don't want to drink at all, but your client orders alcohol, you don't need to underscore your virtue. Simply say, "I'd love to, but I have to spearhead a meeting this afternoon." Or order something very light, along with a soda or mineral water, and let the alcohol sit. When I don't want to drink but think my client would feel uncomfortable with his or her drink if I don't have one, I order a bitter aperitif and soda and barely touch it.

What food to order at a power meal depends on a number of factors, the most important being timing, and secondly how difficult your selection is to eat.

Imagine that your client orders a chef's salad, which is a mound of lettuce, meats and cheeses requring more than one hundred bites to consume. You want to order the scampi, which is four broiled shrimp. What you want is an eight-bite meal, and your client wants a one hundred-bite meal. Unless you plan to do nearly all of the talking, you will wind up with a poorly timed power lunch. Your plate could be whisked away while your client has some seventy-five bites remaining on his plate. Your simple ordering mistake could cause your client to feel rushed through a meal you've planned in order to spend a leisurely time together.

To avoid timing problems, practice the art of the bite count. Determine what to order if you planned to hold 65 percent of the conversation at a meal, leaving your client with 35 percent of the conversation time, and vice versa.

Regardless of their bite content, such difficult-to-eat menu items as ribs and crayfish should always be avoided (if it comes with a bib, there's your clue) unless the point of the meal is to "get down and dirty" with a client who enjoys informality and may have thought your previous encounters too stiff.

Even a pasta dish can be dangerous, as one candidate learned while interviewing for a job. Right at the point of salary negotiation, this woman hung pasta from a fork. Then, as it dangled over her lower lip, and a piece fell into her lap, the hiring manager asked her her salary requirement, and she fell apart.

Many of the sins I see today are pasta-related. Why order it at a business meal if you have not been trained in how to eat it? I always feel more comfortable with pasta that fits neatly on the flat surface of my fork—tortellini, for example.

As important as the entree's bite count and content is its pronunciation. Nationwide, people regularly embarrass themselves and their dining partners by butchering the pronunciation of French menu items.

We feel pronunciation is so important, in fact, to power entertaining and a professional image that we have developed the Sales Athlete® French Menu Interpreter. If French menus are a problem for you, send a stamped self-addressed envelope to The Sales Athlete®, 9808 Wilshire Boulevard, Beverly Hills, CA 90212. We'll send you a free interpreter.

Armed with the assurance that comes from knowing how to order a meal and which fork to use, your next challenge is setting up, getting through and ending a power meal. The cardinal rule for any power meal: Never entertain in a restaurant you have not tried first.

Become a restaurant critic. Try new places,

make yourself known to the maitre d', familiarize yourself with the menu and make a list of the restaurant's "power tables."

Power tables are those offering the most privacy and comfort. Ideally, look for a booth or a corner table where you and your client can sit kitty-corner from each other. Avoid "secretarial tables"—those tables for two jammed together in a line where everyone can hear the conversation at the next table—and "lover's tables"—banquettes designed for couples sitting side by side.

Most restaurants have for their own use diagrams of seating arrangements, with each table numbered. If you are going to be entertaining at a restaurant, ask for the diagram ahead of time and refer to it when making reservations so you can request a table by its number. "Table number four" is specific, while "a nice window table" could lead you to a table where you're practically on the lap of adjacent diners.

Remember that a major point of power entertaining is to make your client feel respected, well cared for and comfortable in your company. Sometimes you can advance that feeling by entertaining lavishly at the most elegant restaurant in town. Other times, you may want to bring a chummy quality to a relationship that has been too stuffy to establish the kind of trust needed for closing major sales.

One sales athlete I know went so far as to totally outfit himself for a duck hunt with his most important client. This urbanite was fundamentally opposed to hunting, but nevertheless seized a rare opportunity to cement a relationship with his client in the wild.

He awoke before dawn and climbed into a tiny boat with a flannel-clad bank president. "The wind was blasting at my face. My lips were frozen," he recalled, grimacing.

He slogged gamely into the marsh, up to his chest in rubber waders. He waited for the ducks. Hours later, a single duck appeared. He raised his gun and shot, realizing only after the smoke cleared that he and the bank president had bonded. They'd shot the same duck.

Power entertaining generally falls into five more mundane categories—breakfast, lunch, dinner, cocktails and "events." Breakfast is my favorite for straight business. It is inexpensive, doesn't involve alcohol and is often easier to schedule with busy executives than lunch or dinner.

My most successful entertaining involves bringing together longtime clients with new clients or client prospects in a setting or at an event where I have arranged every detail to ensure client confidence and a great time.

I like attending and supporting industry charity events such as races at which employees seek donations for each mile run or company softball games. They give you the opportunity to spend time with executives of the corporation as you cheer employees on, and to support good causes in the process.

Here is how I planned two different events to meet the needs of my clients and at the same time promote goodwill toward my business.

A group of clients were visiting Los Angeles from Atlanta and New York with their wives. To ask them to meet socially without their wives would create an uncomfortable situation—they would be forced to refuse the invitation or leave their wives on their own in a strange town. Instead, I invited them all to a tour of "my" Los Angeles. Two of the finest young contemporary artists in California, Judy Stabile and Philip Slagter, and well-known chef Claude Segall agreed to open their lofts and kitchen to my clients.

When it was over, everyone was happy. The clients enjoyed a great California brunch and an inside look at the work of my two artists—all as a backdrop to their business discussions and insights into how the Sales Athlete® Program could increase their sales coast to coast.

In the same week, I hosted thirty clients to a "Queen's Supper." Using invitations attached to costume tiaras for the women, and formal bow ties for the men, I invited seven loyal, longtime clients and seven new or prospective clients and their spouses to a celebration at Trader Vic's, identical to the supper enjoyed by Queen Elizabeth as the guest of President Reagan on her visit to California. The occasion was the celebration of my tenth year of serving clients in Los Angeles.

At a dinner like this, my client fans do the cheerleading for my business with client prospects. Satisfied clients can tell client prospects about the success they've enjoyed with my firm, and about how our relationship has developed over the years. If you've taken good care of your clients over the years, they will give you good public relations in return.

Mind you, both of these examples of "power entertaining" were planned outside of my usual office hours. They involved attention to many details, but did not leave me feeling pressured or harried. Because my time management system allows me to see my schedule clearly and to adjust my priorities, I am frequently able to plan several events for entertaining clients without taking time from my normal work schedule. Properly planned, all of them are fun, not just work.

One of my favorite examples of taking care of clients, taking care of business and having a terrific time all at the same time occurred one Bastille Day. We reserved a table for ten at Le Dome in Los Angeles, which has fabulous food and attracts an eclectic crowd.

The prospects I invited to dinner were the president of a neurological service, a real estate developer, a network executive and the human resources officer of a bank, along with their spouses. We asked several clients to come by after dinner for coffee and cognac to celebrate Bastille Day, so the party for ten became a party for sixteen. As it turned out, other clients were at other tables, so there was table-hopping and dancing all around.

It was a glitzy, memorable evening for us all, and one during which I did quite a bit of business—all in a relaxed, effortless manner. The real estate developer had previously refused to look at training for his people, hiring only experienced people so he wouldn't have to train them. I noticed as I called his office several times that his salespeople were in serious need of telephone sales training. I could have made a few more sales calls on this prospect and I'm sure I would have made headway, but it was his sitting next to the neurosurgeon who had used my training services that led to his seeking my help.

The neurosurgeon was convinced my training of his front-line sales staff had changed the tone of his practice to one that inspired trust. The bank officer, meanwhile, sold the network executive on the value of our training services. These accounts matured because our seating arrangement placed clients of our service between two prospects. Even if it hadn't worked out so fortuitously, we still would have enjoyed the evening, and the goodwill generated by the occasion would remain with these prospects the next time I called on them.

Sales athletes respect the fact that their clients are as busy as they are, so they take pains to create occasions in which everyone can truly relax without feeling pulled away from important work.

Taking care of your clients may involve helping them to network with other clients, friends or services regardless of whether you are present. It is terrible to go to a city and not know anyone, for instance. If a client calls me and says, "I'm going to St. Louis for the first time—what do you know about it?" I want to be sure that this client is well taken care of when he arrives there.

I advise the client to do as I do when I want to entertain clients in an unfamiliar city: Call ahead to the concierge of the hotel and ask if they have a limousine service that can be rented by the hour at a reasonable rate. Then call that service, speak to the manager and find out whether he can provide a tour of the city for a reasonable charge. Next, ask for the names of the city's premier clubs and restaurants—not tourist spots, but the exclusive (and frequently private) clubs. Contact those clubs and introduce yourself by telephone to the owner or maitre d'.

Once in town take the limo tour, stopping off at the clubs and restaurants to establish personal rapport with the owners and maitre d's. Decide which establishment offers the best menu and atmosphere for your business entertaining.

My clients are delighted with the plan. Not only do they get a good overview of a strange city, they are able to entertain clients there confidently. They are grateful to me for helping to encourage loyalty with their own clients.

The opportunity to extend a loyal hand to clients may occur in situations entirely unrelated to the business you do with each other. Embrace such opportunities gratefully—they will enable you to establish deeper bonds of loyalty.

One of my clients called to tell me her two

children were denied access to a prestigious preschool in town. As it turned out, the wife of one of my most satisfied clients is the director of that preschool. Neither of these two women had remembered it, but they had met before at a large gathering at my home. I called the director and said, "Remember that wonderful woman who played the cello and was in advertising? She left the party early because her children were with a babysitter," etc.

After that conversation, the two children were granted another interview in a more relaxed setting, and both were granted admission.

What does all of this have to do with business? You can't be certain that such favors or gestures will win contracts. If, however, none of these people did business with me because something about my service didn't fit their needs at the time, I would at least be certain of getting a hearing the next time an opportunity came up. And the relationships I have nurtured would give me an opportunity to develop programs that *do* fit their needs.

Similarly, entertaining gives me an opportunity to ask questions in a relaxed atmosphere, so I can customize my presentation to the fullest advantage of my client or prospect. If, for whatever reason, my service doesn't fit, at least they would know my intentions were to meet their needs, and I would enjoy a hearing the next time an opportunity came up for us to do business.

Entertaining clients you know can also give you the kind of access that you would not get cold-calling over the telephone or in the prospect's office. Mingling business with social events in this way gives you an opportunity to find out what is really on clients' and prospects' minds, and to build a presentation that addresses their real needs.

Sales athletes look for every opportunity to do business under such relaxed, quasi-social circumstances. They spend most of their time networking within their clients' industries, not their own. In other words, if you are representing a product to the financial community, your priority should be on developing your relationships in the associations that involve bankers—wherever you might meet clients and learn more about their needs—before you'd attend a meeting of financial sales representatives like yourself. I support both, but would not choose my own industry's organizations to the exclusion of clients'.

You can also promote your company in a variety of ways at the trade shows and conventions of client industries. For the cost of an insurance policy, you can offer a $55,000 Cadillac as a prize from your company to anyone making a hole-in-one at an industry golf tournament. (The insurance company will insure against the odds of anyone winning a hole-in-one.) Advertise in the event magazine your prize and challenge to anyone who makes a hole-in-one. Everyone will have a good time at the golf tournament, everyone will get a chance at the Cadillac—and you will have bonded your company's name to the grand prize.

You can donate your product or services as the prize for industry association raffles, or donate a reasonably priced item to a charity for promotional value. You'll be supporting an industry need, you'll be supporting all members equally and you'll be putting something back into the industry that is supporting your own company. Of course, you would select for donations items of quality that are in keeping with the image of your organization.

No one cares how much you know until they know how much you care. Sales athletes look for opportunities to show clients that they care and want to build a positive relationship with their companies.

In developing close relationships in business, I have been able to design my services to fit my clients perfectly. My service has been developed over the years through the help of people who care enough to say, "You may not want to do it this way—I really like this part, but I think your service would be better if you'd consider . . ." That kind of relationship is born out of trust. It takes time and nurturing.

Simple, thoughtful gestures that take very little time and effort on your part can also set you apart from your competition and cement a business relationship with loyalty. You don't have to "remember" birthdays, anniversary dates and children's graduations—you simply have to write them down once in your time management system. When the date arrives, all it takes is a phone call to deliver a special basket of out-of-season fruit, to send flowers or the perfect card or to surprise your client with a congratulatory meal.

The creative "buffers" against rejection we referred to in Chapter 3 can also be used to keep your loyal clients in good shape. Imaginative or outstanding sales aids you have chosen to woo new clients should also be used for remembering and caring for long-term client relationships.

The dynamics of loyalty are based upon establishing trust, and the consistency of earning that trust. With our clients, we have an agreement for what we did yesterday. We don't have an agreement about tomorrow. Tomorrow has to be based upon our relationship now. Five years from now, we could do wonderful things together, but we can't predict whether or not we will for sure. We might intend or desire it, but in order to make it happen, we need to work at keeping the excitement and trust we have developed alive.

The company of a client I had for ten years was bought by another company, which had its own in-house sales training staff. My client wants to do business with our company but can't because she must acclimate herself to her new corporation. She telephoned me, asking me to be patient with her over the next year or so. It was a kind and loyal gesture. We may do business again five years from now, or we may not, but between now and five years hence we will do things together to keep that trust.

Louis B. Mayer handed Will Rogers a thick contract to sign at the height of his career. Rogers flipped over the contract and wrote on the back of it, "I work, you pay." That was the agreement that bound them, and they lived together happily ever after.

Loyalty in business is not slick, like planning and scheduling—it is transient and requires trust. Loyalty is the foundation of the sales athlete's career.

The Equipment of a Sales Athlete

From the lists of sales athletes nationwide, here is the equipment that will help you keep your competitive edge.

THE SELLING SYSTEM
Software to help you manage client and prospect files and obtain more accurate revenue projections.
Pyramid Software, Inc.
22691 Lambert Street, Suite 506
El Toro, CA 92630
(714) 583-1060

THE COMPLETE PC
A PC-based fax, scanner and phone machine, particularly useful for the salesperson with no home-base personnel.
521 Cottonwood
Milpitas, CA 95035
(408) 434-0145

VISUAL TELEPHONE

Transmits black-and-white visual images of anything held in front of it. Not a fully developed technology as of this printing, it may soon have applications in business.

Loma Telecom
1070 Arques Avenue
Sunnyvale, CA 95054
(408) 746-2030

PLANTRONICS CORDLESS EARPIECE

An essential for people who spend a lot of time on the phone.

Plantronics
345 Encinal
Santa Cruz, CA 95065
(408) 426-6060

MESSAGE SOFTWARE

The Forget-Me-Not software is installed on your PC to deliver messages to you at set times.

Sterling Castle Software
702 Washington Street, Suite 174
Marina Del Rey, CA 90292
(213) 306-3020

VIDEOTRAX COPIER
This copies information from disks to videotapes, a space- and money-saving convenience.
Alpha Micro
3501 Sunflower
Santa Ana, CA 92704
(714) 957-8500

THE FAXSWITCH
A switching system that routes one phone line into your handset or fax, whichever is needed to avoid costly separate phone lines.
Vada Systems, Inc.
9329 Douglas Drive
Riverside, CA 92503
(714) 687-2492

ACT! SALES DATABASE
A database, word processor and more. For about $10, the company will send you a videotape demonstrating the product and some sample disks.
Conductor Software, Inc.
92080 W. Royal Lane
Irving, TX 75063
(214) 929-4749

ETAK ELECTRONIC AUTO NAVIGATOR

Historically used by ambulances and firetrucks, these electronic maps are now manufactured for individual use in a limited number of cities. They show alternative routes to specific destinations and can slash the time you spend covering a territory.

Etak, Inc.
1455 Adams Drive
Menlo Park, CA 94025
(415) 328-3825

ELECTRONIC MAIL

Sends messages, contracts and business letters by PC.

MCI Mail
2000 M Street NW
Washington, DC 20036
(202) 293-4225

TIME/DESIGN MANAGEMENT SYSTEM

A planning and scheduling tool that increases productivity and peace of mind.

Time/Design
11835 West Olympic Blvd. Suite 450
Los Angeles, CA 90064
(800) 637-9942